GUERRILLA BUSINESS 2.0

PRACTICAL ADVICE, UNIQUE MARKETING IDEAS, AND BUSINESS MANAGEMENT SUGGESTIONS FOR THE COTTAGE & SMALL BUSINESS OWNER

HEATH D. ALBERTS

DIGITAL NINJAS MEDIA, INC.

Library of Congress cataloging in publication data applied for.

ISBN-13: 978-1508582205
ISBN-10: 1508582203

FIRST EDITION – Published – 04/01/12
SECOND EDITION – Published 02/21/15

15   16   17   18   19 ❖ OV/RRD   10   9   8   7   6   5   4   3   2

For Dave Klingenmeyer,
Gary Naser, and Kim Kowalewski,
without whose unique, individual,
mentoring this book would not exist.

"Just because you can, doesn't mean that you should.
And just because you can't, doesn't mean that you shouldn't try."
Heath D. Alberts

Foreword

Over the years, I have been employed in a number of occupations and positions - both full and part time, vertical and horizontal*. In fact, there was a time when I juggled a full time job, three part-time jobs, and some circular saws all at once (okay, maybe I'm embellishing just a wee bit). I guess that one could safely state with some surety that I was – and remain - a workaholic. Or crazy - I don't know. A lot of people say things to me that I don't listen to, unless it's in Haiku form. Then I'm all ears, for some odd reason.

*(I'm kidding on that last bit – as far as you know, anyway.)

Fifteen years ago, I was asked by a long-time friend to accept a position at a machine shop that he had recently opened. That positon evolved into that of the Operations Manager, in present day. While his expertise in the fields of machining, machine repair, and mechanics were beyond copious, I didn't know thing one about running the day-to-day operations of a functioning machine shop.

What I knew was this: as a friend and co-worker of my Father, this individual had offered me my first job when I was twelve years old, in what was then a cottage, custom woodworking business. I had remained in this position, on and off, part-time, for a number of years and watched as his product's quality and craftsmanship blew the competition out of the water. Time and time again, he would attend a craft fair or show, and return having been profoundly successful. I came to the realization early on that here was an individual who knew what it took to turn a profit, and make a business work - especially when he knew and understood the product. Suffice it to say, I took the job, and my life changed forever.

As the business grew, both He and I grew with it. We learned a lot of hard lessons, made a lot of tough decisions, made even more stupid mistakes, and suffered a lot of hardship. At times, his acumen and skills were all that kept the budding company in forward motion. Over the years, it grew from a three-man show in a garage workshop, to a nationally recognized, thirty-individual, multi-million dollar business enterprise. Over the span of those fifteen years, we have always turned a profit. This occurred even when times were toughest, and other businesses in our sector were closing their doors.

The reason?

A lot of it has to do with our collective abilities, precipitated upon hiring smart, and 'training up' to higher echelon positions. Certainly quality, communications, timeliness, and price are all factors as well. Yet - all things being equal - the one pivotal point that went above and beyond to set our company apart was that we learned on the fly, put in place systems to nullify repetition of negatives, and remembered all too well our mistakes. It is these learning experiences, and the ideas spawned from their having occurred, that I intend to share with you. To some, they may seem obvious; to others, a little insane. It doesn't matter what you think about the ideas, because I know this to be true: they work - all of them. I've seen them proven out in real-life situations.

Further, this book is different. Many books dealing specifically with the subject of Guerrilla *Marketing* offer a smattering of excellent tips, but then peter out somewhere in the twenty-tip range, and become either too specific or repetitious. I have personally attempted to get away from this phenomena in an effort to offer you genuinely useful ideas that fall not only into the Guerrilla *Marketing* category, but also into the realms of what I have dubbed Guerrilla *Business* practices. Some are old, some are new, some are new twists on old principles, and those of which I am most proud are results of my own personal efforts.

Finally, you will find recommended reading, as well as business and management principles.

Why business and management principles in a book containing marketing ideas?

Believe it or not, tying in business and management is far more germane to the larger marketing picture than you might initially realize.

Fair warning: this book is written in an unusual manner, in that it does not read like a novel. It is, at its core, a series of unique monologues that may be read individually or all at once (skipping around at random hurts nothing, in this case). Also, please understand that it is incumbent upon you - the reader - to make certain that in implementing any of the ideas herein, that you do not violate any local, regional, state, or federal laws, covenants, prohibitions, or decrees by doing so.

So sit down, curl up with something warm to drink, and consider for a few moments your business, as it is right now. Then clear you head, and imagine your business invoking some or all of the forthcoming ideas. I promise that there is something in here for everyone, and hopefully a whole host of things that you've never considered before.

Heath D. Alberts
March 3rd, 2012

Part 1: Personal & Consumer Psychology

Lower Prices Mean... More Profits?

Your competition is ever-changing. Sometimes there's a new shark in the tank. At other times, one disappears silently into oblivion after losing the battle in the business world. The world of business, as a collective whole, experiences ebb and flow like this all the time. The truly great companies - the companies who are on top for a good long time - are in such a position for good reason.

Often, one of these reasons is the ability to adapt to situations beyond their sphere of control, in an effort to bring them (at least somewhat) closer to a manageable state.

This is where we begin the cited thought: *Lower Prices Means More Profits*. It sounds overly simple; perhaps even a bit silly. In my personal experience, however, you'd be amazed at how many business owners and employees don't understand the concept. Or worse, are unwilling to even hear it. I hope that you'll be different.

The concept, at its core, looks something like this:

Let's suppose that you charge $50.00 per hour for a service. This is the rate at which you make optimum profit, while still providing value and covering expenses.

In reality, every business has what is known as a 'Burden Rate'. Burden rates are the base numbers for inevitable expenses that your business *must* achieve compensation for prior to profit occurring. Included in the burden rate are things like rent, utilities, wages, insurance, taxes, stock of product – all things that you need to have paid for in order make the business go on the most basic level. Once the burden rate is covered, then profit begins to occur.

When you began your business, you ran all of these numbers, and figured out the balancing point between profit and value to the customer. If you didn't, then I'm totally slapping your knuckles with a ruler, virtually, right now, while doing my best shrieking nun impression. The great businesses will be able to realize when it is appropriate to tip this scale to one side or another.

On one hand, we have the volume versus return theory. This states that you can achieve more business, if you're willing to be somewhat flexible on pricing (coupons and sales do this all the time). For example:

A customer comes to you and says that they cannot afford $50.00 per hour for your services, but they still wish to do business with you.

A lot of businesses would just walk away at this point, because this person is not willing or able to meet their stated pricing structure.

Me?

I'd ask what fits their budget model better, before I just dismiss them.

Let's say they compel you to understand that $40.00 per hour is all that they can manage.

Now you have a decision to make.

Specifically, how does the $40.00 per hour stack up against your burden rate, and your in-house workload, at any given moment. If your burden rate is $21.00 per hour, then you stand to make $19.00 per hour in profit from this venture.

This transaction, therefore, would meet your criteria for providing profit.

Next you have to consider whether this is worth your time or not. If you're low on work, then having $19.00 per hour may be a better choice in the short-term than demanding a full $29.00, but not having enough work to fill all time available.

Perhaps you can even give this work to a subordinate employee (who makes a lower wage than you), instead of doing it yourself.

This is where knowing your burden rate is so crucial, because it allows a level of nimble-ness and flexibility in your business model that will allow you to continue turning a profit, even during leaner times.

Conversely, and much more difficult to find, is the opposite situation. If a customer needs something 'rush' or needs a special service that you don't normally offer, don't dismiss this either!

'Rush' services and un-offered services should be right in your wheelhouse. And those services need to carry a premium.

I once had a tooling vendor (and dear friend) tell me a story about a buyer from an aircraft manufacturer that called her. He needed a thousand clay poker chips for an upcoming event, and didn't have the time to find them.

Know what she did?

She found them, bought them, marked them up, and got them to him. Her company made an above-average profit, and she became that much more essential as a business contact for that guy.

Where I work (i.e. - my day job) we do this sort of thing all the time. It's what keeps us in the fore of our customer's minds, because we're not afraid of (just about) anything, and they can go to one shop (us) to have all of their needs (insane or not) fulfilled on one purchase order.

Rush services should also be assessed on a case-by-case basis. Is the customer willing to pay an extra X% to get it this week, instead of waiting in line?

And if so, can you deliver on this, without disrupting your normal flow of business?

Services that are 'associated' - loosely, or otherwise - with your business can also be considered. At *Digital Ninjas Media, Inc.*, we offer services that are, in fact, 'second-tier'. This means that we don't do the work ourselves (completely, or partially). Rather, we sub-source it to a vendor who is better equipped and skilled to do it.

Sound like a rip off?

A lot of folks think like this. But here's the cold reality: we've taken the time, effort, and energy to *find* and *vet* someone who does what it is that you want done. We're taking all of the risk of getting it done, to your specifications, and in your selected time frame. We also take all the risk in paying for the service, before you pay us.

And best of all?

You only need to deal with one company, so there's no collaboration or chasing things down. This has value.

In your business model, I would recommend considering what 'subcontracting' you can do. Then, I would consider an upcharge percentage on to that vendor's pricing for your time and trouble. I usually recommend a *minimum* of 10%. If you can't get 10%, it's probably not worth the hassle (but make certain of that, before you decline!)

On the other side of the line, there's overt greed. Don't get greedy, either. Be fair. Treat your customer's money as you would your own. Being a vendor is, at its core, a fiduciary responsibility borne upon your business out of trust from your customers. Never betray that trust.

So remember: sometimes more business, at a lesser price, is better than none at all. And never dismiss out of hand 'subcontracting' or 'rush' work. They provide a unique opportunity to make additional money, and are not a nuisance to be dismissed!

Know Your Burden Rate

Burden Rate (n): The amount of money that a business is required to earn each week/month/year before a profit is turned.

As we've touched on in the last segment, the burden rate of a business is something that you *must* be cognizant of, lest you be destined to fail. By comprehending your burden rate, you can begin to determine where cost savings can occur, where money is being lost (often unnecessarily) and where your business is headed.

Since we've already touched on that aspect of it, I wanted to take today to take it a step further: What are your employees costing you?

Employees are, at their heart a necessary evil, or a joyous burden, depending on your perspective. For me, they're a double-edged sword. For each one hired, you're banking on the premise that they will have the skill, ambition, drive, and desire to fulfill their end of the bargain to the best of their ability, thereby making them more valuable come raise time.

But how many of us are truly able to put a number on what each employee brings to the table?

The answer might both surprise, and depress you. Here's how you do it:

Each employee has a salary or hourly wage. Prior to each employee's annual review (and if you're not doing this, then shame on you to begin with - you're practically asking for failure, or mediocrity at best), calculate all of the known quantities.

- Wages and bonuses over a 52-week period
- Federally mandated taxes that you contribute on their behalf (Social Security, Medicare, FUTA, and State Unemployment)
- Benefits: Your portion of any and all benefits paid out to the employee (Insurance premiums, profit sharing, company-sponsored events, etc.)
- Any sick days, personal days, or vacation days that have accrued, but have not been used (including their impact on the above numbers!)
- Lost revenue due to non-presence (i.e. – when an employee has not been at your place of business, for one reason or another, and someone has had to cover for them, or they have not contributed to the productivity/billable bottom line due to their actions.) This is *especially* egregious when an employee who can provide billable hours is forced into a position of non-billable hours. They're not only working far below their capacity, they're costing you money in lost revenue and productivity.
- Lost revenue due to error (i.e. – we log all of the quantifiable errors that each employee makes at the machine shop that I run. I calculate the lost revenue in both times, material, and outside services, then triple the labor number. The reason? As mentioned earlier in this book, you've lost the initial time to make the product (1x), you've had to re-make the product (2x), and the time spent to re-make the product was not permitted to make something new that would otherwise be billable (3x)
- Workman's compensation insurance for that category per hour
- Any number of specialized facets that may occur in your business (i.e. – employee discounts vs. their purchases with said-same, et cetera.)

The first number that will *astound* you will come from businesses where production of billable hours/goods is in play. If they're an employee who produces 'billable' hours, every hour that they are not present has a negative impact far greater than their sick pay, vacation pay, etc. Unfortunately, this needs to be considered in the Burden Rate.

I recommend developing a spreadsheet template so that you can copy and plug-in employees through the review cycle each year. You may also wish to figure operating expenses that pertain to the employee as well. In my case (managing a machine shop), I can safely figure a portion of the utilities, tooling, raw materials, etc. into the mix, if I so choose. But don't choose to do this lightly, either.

What you find will startle you, but is also a good tool for proving or disproving the employee's true worth. Often, business owners have no notion of what a 'good' or 'bad' employee really is. Sure, they might miss a lot of work but they're super-productive when they're there, so that makes up for it... right?

No, not usually. By running these numbers, you can come to a number of your own: what it costs you to employ this person, per annum. Once this number is quantified, things can become a little vague.

If you're in a production environment, then it's simple. Multiply the number of hours worked by the amount you charge for those hours. Then compare it to your Burden Rate calculation. If there's a decent profit there, then it might be time for a raise: a raise that comes with the expectation that, this time next year, that number will be relatively similar or even marginally better.

Conversely, if the number comes up the other way, that employee that you perceived as great (or even just okay) has just proven otherwise. Here, you now have a decision to make, depending on the egregiousness of the offset. You may choose to show the employee these numbers, explaining *why* you cannot afford that raise they feel that they deserve. You can also use this as a tool to discuss areas for improvement with the employee, all while being able to *show* them the financial impacts of their actions.

I see, time and time again, businesses that have a few stellar employees, who buoy one or many weaker ones. Some are actually costing the company far more than they're worth to retain. But, since no one's checked the Burden Rates, nothing is ever done about it.

I then, often, see the business owner making a second mistake: telling the employees that there's no money for raises. Lax employees probably won't care. They often know how good they've got it. The mediocre ones will probably get cranky and deter your profit margins a little more. The good ones will be savvy enough to realize the stupidity in that remark without a Burden Rate foundation, and walk away.

How do I know this?

I know because I myself, and my wife as well, have departed a number of jobs for just this reason. We also hire a lot of these folks at my shop, when they walk away from other shops not performing this function.

As employees, we get tired of hearing what essentially amounts to the fact that we're being evaluated by vagary. Or, worse still, nothing more solid than, 'We didn't make enough profit for raises', even though we know there is Burden Rate being wasted, needlessly. We're the folks you want to keep around. Ironically, we're also the ones that are the least likely to stay on to continue to support the employment-needy around us. We're the ones that you won't fight to keep until it's too late to do so.

Think I'm being overly simplistic?

Perhaps I am. But consider the fact of how well your business has done, versus how well you *feel* it should have done. Consider how many good employees you've seen move on, because you, 'Couldn't afford to pay them those high wages they were asking for.' Think of how many employees have been with you for years, and where you feel their value is on a scale from one to ten.

In other words: take a big boy/girl pill. Take responsibility for your potential mismanagement, and rectify it by doing yourself the service of developing this Burden Rate technique. Then, implement it - immediately.

I GUARANTEE (note the all caps, there) that your business can be more profitable, without my being the evil, money-grubbing ogre you're probably thinking that I am right now.

I'm not. You'll see.

I, as an employee, simply want to be paid what I'm worth, in reference to my peers, in a business that is well run so that my hard work will result not in financial crutches for my weaker co-workers, but grander things for myself, and the for company.

You can often easily spot your highest producers. They're the ones who you rely on the most, who you force to do the top-tier work – so that you know that it's done right. They're the ones you trust. And they're probably also the ones you ride the hardest.

These types of employees don't usually mind that sort of 'go-to' treatment. Some may even thrive on it. However, they do begin to look for greener pastures once they spot inconsistencies in treatment that is not commensurate with wage values, or Burden Rate comparisons.

If you choose to ignore the above advice, you will find yourself churning through the occasional stellar employee, while also finding yourself surrounded in permanence with the remoras who know a good thing when they get a paycheck from it.

If a stellar employee is ridden too hard, and they suddenly make subtle changes to their demeanor or workday – look out. They're inadvertently telling you that since you've given up on them, they're giving up on you. And two-week's notice won't be far behind, as some other savvy employer snatches them up, to leave you floundering with the group they once bolstered.

Humor me. DO THIS (note the all caps again). And if I'm wrong, you let me know.

Unleash Your Inner Guerrilla

In case you haven't noticed, Guerrilla Marketing isn't always easy. In fact for me, it often runs well outside of my comfort zone. It offers insane, zany, and weird ways to get the attention of folks around you who probably have no idea who in the hell you are. And to some, like myself, this is counter-intuitive. In fact, I prefer to be as low profile as possible. Or at least, I did. Until:

After ten years of dragging my feet, making excuses, fearing judgment, and being embarrassed, I published my first book. And if you want to talk about a very personal experience, that one ranks right up there. I put a piece of myself out for the world at large to have its way with. To market it, I had to put even more of myself out.

What I discovered along the way is this: you can't care what individuals think, unless they've been true friends, in a meaningful way, for a substantial period of time. Then - and only then - should you consider their specific concern(s). Everyone else hasn't made a difference in your life yet, so they haven't earned the right to be heard in an introspective manner.

You have to let your ego go, when it comes to criticism from those folks, though. It's *much* easier said than done. Believe me. I know.

Am I glad that I did it?

Yes. Though over the ten years that have elapsed since writing the thing, my writing has become stronger, my sense of space in a story has become more intuitive, and I realize now that the book was never really the 'slam-dunk' that I had deluded myself into believing that it was. It was pretty crappy by my current standards.

Even so, I sent it off into the world.

Back to Guerrilla Marketing: it is a harsh mistress. I won't even sugarcoat it. Very few people are the types of free spirits who just dive into it and feel like they're finding something, rather than losing it.

To you folks, I say that this is one time where I wish that I were you.

But, I'm not.

So I closed my eyes, told myself I could do this, kept my true friends close, and just put the book out there.

And you know what?

It wasn't that bad, once I set that ground rule.

In fact, I found that after months of discomfort and struggle, there was more positive feedback than negative*.

*(Which hurt, but not too much when I considered the source and remembered my rule).

I can't guarantee that this will be your experience, but I can tell you this: I would be a lesser person if I had deprived myself of those moments of pride and elation that comes from individuals genuinely pleased with my work. The result was a positive learning experience, and a confidence builder.

So break out of that mold that is 'you today'. And become that 'you tomorrow' that's stuck in there. It's worth it. I promise.

26   **You Are Boring: Fix That**

"Me, me, me, is dull, dull, dull."

I don't remember where I initially read this, but it's something that's always stuck with me.

If you want to network your business more successfully, then it's a good idea to start by opening yourself up to being networked *to*. If you are initially interested in others, they are more receptive to what you might have to say. It takes an investment in time, but it works a great deal better than walking up to a stranger and spouting off about how awesome your product is.

**Do Your Views Of Yourself Jibe
With Those Of Your Employees/Employer?**

Before you answer that, let's discuss it a bit.

I recently read a humorous quote that stated something akin to, *'95% of Americans believe that they're smarter than the other 95%.'* I'm assuming that the other 5% are either lying, nuns, clinically brain dead individuals, or politicians.

I wanted to move on with my life after reading that little nugget of truth, yet found that I just couldn't. It got me thinking. I mean it *really* got me thinking.

Why?

Because if I was being honest, I felt like I really *was* smarter than most Americans. My guess is that you might as well.

The problem?

Someone has to be wrong. And, sad as it might be, it might just be you and I.

"All right," you might say, "you've got me to read this book, you tell me something I already knew about how awesome I am, and then turn it around on me in a total jerk move.

What's your point, you douche-weasel?"

My point is this: you are not as great as you think you are. And this goes for employers and employees alike.

But it's okay!

This is a workable situation!

Let's begin tackling the problem from the employer's side (but – employees – read along!)

As an employer, you are responsible for all of the risk in owning the business: insurance, workman's compensation, taxes, paying the bills, creating the work, maintaining workload, forecasting, keeping the shareholders happy, and eight thousand other things that would make most mortals opt to investigate the business end of a skunk with their tongue rather than do what you're doing.

In some ways, you're a modern-day superhero.

Employers, however, often focus too much on these points and forget one additional, key piece of the equation. It's this: while you've done all that, the employees are the fuel that makes the engine run. Without something as seemingly simple as fuel, a *Maserati* is just a pretty lawn ornament. As such, you have an obligation to maximize profit, while also keeping the fuel clean, and the vehicle that is your business road-worthy. And that's a painfully difficult exercise at times.

A great leader (i.e. – the employer) develops relationships with their followers (i.e. – the employees). Oftentimes, a person can have amazing business acumen, yet possess no human interaction skills. And this, sadly, is the death knell for many business ventures. They've literally failed before they've even begun. It's only a matter of time.

Ask yourself this question: do your employees like you?

Are you, in fact, fortunate enough to have employees who are willing to do what it takes to make you happy?

Are your employees committed to the company's well-being, without fail or question?

That's a tough set of questions, isn't it?

Now, I'll ask you this: how many times did you just lie to yourself?

It's okay. You're human. Then again, so are your employees.

As humans, we crave acceptance, recognition, praise, and inclusion. If, as an employer, you can focus on nurturing those human needs (without being overtly disingenuous, as so many bosses and business owners end up being), you will develop a solid crew of workers who would go through Hell and back to make damn sure that your business is the best that it can be. They'll be motivated to be productive, to be resourceful, and to be open and honest. A few kind words, meaningful recognition programs, or the like are sometimes all it takes to make the things your employees say about you when you're not around positive in nature.

Ask yourself this: how often do you hear a friend, relative, or colleague gush on and on about what a jackass, know-nothing tyrant they work for?

Now, to expound upon that, how often do you hear the opposite?

I'm guessing the ratio is phenomenally one-sided.

27

As an employer, you need to recognize a few things that you might not otherwise consider:

- Lost time and motion translates into lost revenues
- Lack of productivity devalues the product or service you're offering with every passing minute
- Lack of employee morale is transmitted directly to your customer base – be it oral or physical. And customers do *not* like dealing with the emotional baggage of others. They've got enough of their own to spare.
- Training a new employee is profoundly expensive, when you consider the lost productivity on the part of both the trainer, and the trainee. Finding new employees can add to the costs as well, with regard to placing ads, holding interviews, reviewing résumés, etc. Not to mention potential errors in job performance, which create waste or unsalable product(s).

Employers: look in the mirror. Be critical. No – be *hyper-critical*. It will pay off. I promise. And for the love of all that's good and holy, stop lying to yourself. You'll thank me for it.

Now, let's flip the switch, and visit the world of the employee.

Welcome!

If you're an employee, then you're fortunate enough to have been selected by a business owner as a trustee of their consolidated risk. They've quite literally put their livelihood (or, a part of it) in your hands.

Holy crap – you have responsibility!

Who knew?

As an employee, you need to consider all of the things outlined above. Remember that employers often aren't working a three-hour day to go home to their champagne-filled pool for bon-bons and lobster. Okay, some might be, but the odds are staggeringly against this being the case – work with me, here. Chances are they've worked themselves stupid and put everything on the line, risking it all, to make their dreams a reality. If you don't know about any of this, then I'd encourage you to ask. I think you'll find your employer is a lot more than they seem, and it might change the way you choose to view and interact with them.

Employers, as a rule, need you. There is, however, an old saying: '*Just because you're necessary, doesn't mean that you're important*'. Which is true, in some respects.

I'd like to perform the same experiment on you, as we did on your employer above. Look in a mirror, and ask yourself what your employer thinks of you. I mean, really and truly – not the Adonis-like, chiseled-featured overlord that you envision yourself to be.

It's a hard question, I know.

As a matter of course, in America, most employees are somewhat to profoundly unhappy with their jobs. Part of the problem, however, is that they blame this on the employer, rather than being introspective about it.

Consider: did the employer hunt you down and beg you to work for them?

Or did you apply to their business?

Ah-ha! I just caught 99.9% of you in a trap of your own making. You can't see it, but I'm laughing maniacally, while pretending to twist my handlebar moustache.

Frankly, it's less satisfying than I thought it would be.

>Sigh<

Oh, well.

>Ahem<

If you applied for the position that you now hold, then who do you have to blame?

Often, employees take out their frustrations on their employers using what psychologists call 'transference'. Whether it be their home life, their love life, their regrets, their poor life decisions, their having been screwed-over by someone, etc. These, sadly, are often transposed upon our employers as somehow being their fault. Which is the epitome of unfairness.

Likewise, employers can sometimes do this to their employees. It's a phenomena I like to call 'poisoning the well', because it tends to begin with one individual, and, like a cancer, spread amongst everyone in the workplace.

I could write about this for hours. Which would be awesome for my ego, but sort of unnecessary.

The bottom line is this: every day that you arrive at your place of business – employer or employee – consider all of your interactions. Be kind. Be thoughtful. Be honest. Be forthright. Be fair. And for Pete's sake never *ever* yell or discipline someone in front of others.

Make 'deposits' in the bank of praise, so that when negatives do have to be addressed, they're taken more seriously, and with less stress.

Put yourself in the shoes of others, often. Rescind your initial, gut reaction to situations. Instead, consider them like a crime scene investigator. Often, what appears on the surface to be one thing is, upon analysis and further consideration, quite another. The problem is, most folks don't bother to do the homework. They just go with their gut, open their mouth, and end up being stupid, a dick, or both.

Don't be that person. No one likes that person.

Above all else – be honest with yourself. If we all did more of this, the workplace would be an environment that far fewer of us would dread or vilify.

Know The 'Rule Of 3'

The rule of three is an annoying little bugger. It forces us to face a fact that's unpleasant. So much so that we'd rather kiss our ugly Aunt Edna on that wart on her cheek then face it. Nevertheless, it exists. And it can actually help you.

The Rule of 3 works like this: if your company makes an error, it costs 3x the value of that product or service to make up for the error.

At first, this seems a little ridiculous. And I'll be the first to admit that it doesn't always apply to every business. Even so, it's still relevant, and something you need to consider in your day-to-day operations.

For example:

Let's say that you make custom transmissions for vintage motor scooters. Your employee is working on one, when he accidentally drops it from the lift he's moving it around on. It's a total loss.

This particular transmission was ready to be installed. Now, it's destined to hold your canoe in place while you fish next summer. The price of the transmission was $500.00*.

*(I have no idea what these cost, for the record, and I know as much about motorized vehicles as I do the mating habits of ferrets. Work with me, here, though.)

You have now netted a $500.00 loss, right?

Nope.

You've actually netted a *$1,500.00* loss.

"Did you put LSD in your cereal this morning, Heath?"

Well, no – not *this* morning.

Here's why it's a larger loss than you believe it to be:

- $500.00 in lost revenue
- $500.00 to re-make the thing
- $500.00 in time lost re-making the thing, when you could be profiting from that time

For a small business it might take days, or even weeks, to recover from this loss. As your business grows, or your products become more expensive or complex, accidental losses like this can be debilitating, perhaps even catastrophic to the point of losing the business entirely.

It's important to consider the Rule of 3's, especially when quantifying losses in revenue at the end of the quarters (or year), as well as when it comes time for an employee's review. For as stellar as they might otherwise be, the Rule of 3's could have a huge impact upon their true value to the company.

Sometimes 'Bigger' Doesn't Equate To 'Better'

We've all seen it: the little one-person, Mom-And-Pop business that comes from nowhere, built on sweat, determination, and long hours into a company that employs others and creates a tangible footprint upon the society around it.

Then, often, they grow bigger in an effort to diversify, serve more customers, gain more throughput/output, etc. Sometimes, they stop there. Other times, they continue to the next level, and become a chain, a national force, or even an international force. In effect: something far greater than anyone ever imagined.

Sometimes, this is a good thing. Other times, it's a *great* thing.

The question I want to pose today is: is this the *right* thing?

Here's why I ask:

Recently, one of *Digital Ninjas Media, Inc.'s* clients considered expansion. They wanted to take their business to the next level by purchasing an addition to their building, adding new equipment, and bolstering manpower. We were fortunate enough to be a part of the group-minding behind this process (yep – we're not just pretty faces – we have some business experience too). Initially, we thought that it was a great idea that would make our client a lot more money. That was, until we started thinking not like an observer, but like a researcher.

The decision all began (and ultimately ended) with numbers. First, we collectively developed a business-specific method by which we could 'see' – in a cause and effect manner – how much each employee was bringing to the table in dollar output, versus what it cost the company to employ them. Then we compared it to the employer's perceptions.

And a veritable bomb went off.

So we dug a little deeper. And the more we quantified and monetized the data, the more we found an inversion. In fact, the company was losing money by being as large as it had become already, based on a number of factors that were – to that point – unquantified, or unknown. How did we do this? Here's what we used:

Costs of payroll (including the higher factor of overtime)
Costs of taxes associated with payroll
Costs of unemployment insurance
Costs of employee benefits
Costs of individual errors and mistakes (using the rule of 3)

Next, we took a look at the earnings potential of each employee per hour. Then, we figured out how many hours, on average, they were working in a set period of time. This number, subtracted from the amalgamation of the prior items, showed us what was left over for the company as 'profit'. To the management's surprise, some individuals were actually losing money for the company, while others were clearly carrying it.

The end result?

Expansion seemed like a terrible idea. Downsizing, in fact, would prove to be more profitable.

Now this might sound cruel, or even cold and heartless. But here's the upside: the ownership didn't want anyone to lose their jobs. They truly cared about their employees, as humans first, and employees second (which is something sorely lacking in this day and age). As such, they sat down with each employee, and outlined their findings, as well as setting goals to rectify each individual situation.

In the end, some did, and some did not.

The result, however, was a much stronger and robust workforce. And as a bonus, morale was lifted. The individuals who were shining were further recognized for their stellar contributions.

The company did, in the end, downsize. They changed their business model drastically as well by identifying key areas where cost savings could be achieved, and then tackled each, one by one, in an effort to do so.

Amazingly, as of this writing, we're told that they're doing more with less, and are experiencing a cathartic resurgence in pride of work, employee productivity, and employee recognition. All this occurred because they wanted to expand.

Expansion is something that cannot be, and should not be, taken lightly. If you are considering it, here are some key factors to think about:

- Would you be more profitable and nimble by altering your business model first?

- Would your customers still receive the level of service that they've come to expect from you, or would it potentially suffer?

- Are there enough qualified employees in your area to fill the new positions, while keeping the company workflow moving in a positive way?

- Is the cost of expansion worth the return on investment? Can you quantify it?

- Are you expanding to meet a new need, or just to increase the fulfillment of a current (or future) one?

- Is your company prepared for a 'catastrophic loss' – such as yourself, or your management, in the event of death, departure, or other significant 'acts of God', or force majeure?

- Are you maximizing the potential of all of your current assets – human and physical? Would doing so alleviate the need for expansion?

- Are multiple shifts an option?

- Are you, as the owner, going to be forced to work *in* the business? Or will you be free to work *on* it?

In the end, each business – like each individual – is different. Each one works around a specific model that is right for their industry, locale, economic climate, and any number of other things. I cannot, however, express enough how important it is to quantify everything in the most intuitive manner possible. It affords a snapshot of your company that will (I can almost guarantee) reveal things that you thought you knew which are dead wrong.

Pricing: Pennies Matter

Recently, a friend of mine (Stacy Stateham of *Dragonfly Social,* specifically) got me to thinking about pricing strategy. In fact, as I sat down to write this, I found a second reference (once more, from her) that was freshly posted on *Facebook.*

When I'm doing real work that isn't as fun as this (i.e. - my day job), I spend a good portion of the day bidding tens of thousands of dollars of contract machining work (sometimes more, which is as frightening as it sounds). Over my years on this planet, there are two pricing strategies that I have seen employed that are sort of genius in their own unique ways.

The first, is the commonly known 'law of nines'. The proverbial 'law of nines' states that the human brain is more accommodating to a price of $299 than it is to $301.

Why?

For whatever subconscious reason (and no matter how ridiculous it sounds) our brains tend to 'lessen' the damages when faced with an amount that doesn't break the next base-ten level of pricing. It sounds insane but I'm guessing, if you think about it, you've all done just this (and may still do so even to this day).

This is why many retail chains have employed this strategy in the past (and many still do). *Wal-Mart* bucked that trend by battling *K-Mart* with eights* in the late eighties and early nineties (this was when I was still a part of the red vest army at the sign of the big red "K").

*(They then changed tactics, some time later, and moved to sixes for a bit, as I recall.)

34 Personally?

I used to use the law of nines myself when I was biding work. I would round down on quotations to the next base-ten iteration to a nine. The problem was, most of my competition was doing so as well. After a few years, I got smart, and began asking for customer pricing feedback. And in some cases, customers supplied copious amounts of it. As I scanned the numbers, I found *three* distinctly differing trains of thought:

The most prominent was the obvious tactic: the 'law of nines'. After reviewing this data, I made the immediate decision to go with the *Wal-Mart* method of bumping down to eights.

The results were immediate.

The second tactic was just random: individuals who were quoting the jobs that I was, who were literally using whatever number was spat out (i.e. - $293.00). This can be good for your bottom line, but seems to confuse or consternate the minds of many buyers (I have no idea why). I immediately threw that one out, for good or ill, on most bidding. The exception arose when components were too small on margin to use the law of 9's or the law of 8's, and instead required actual pricing, like that mentioned here.

The third was a more interesting tactic, that I had never considered a whole lot. I dubbed it the 'loose change' theory. Specifically, the individuals quoting would quote not only in dollars, but in random cents as well. On the surface, this seemed, well, stupid.

Who cares about .32 cents in this day and age?

Yet I took a mental step back and thought about it. After a few moments of considering it from all angles, a figurative light bulb went off. To this day, I still use this method *only* on rare occasions where I feel it makes the most sense (like large, assembly-cluster, type quotations).

Why?

Because no matter what the cents behind that decimal point amount to, it gives the appearance that you have analyzed the bid down to the penny. You've been meticulous, you've bid everything perfectly, and in doing so you have overtly looked out for your client to the very best of your human ability.

Personally, I think that's a load of... well, anyway, suffice it to say that I don't necessarily buy it. But what it does to the human mind, is it plants that very seed (subconscious, or otherwise). And on that level, it's a brilliant strategy.

The best advice that I can offer to wrap this section up: find out *everything* that you can about how your competition is bidding or pricing. Look for patterns that you can exploit, and then undermine that system. It might take dropping to rounded-down fours, but the return on awarded jobs, or sales, should be enough for you to suck up the random loss of a few bucks and shop the value meal drive-through for lunch instead of indulging in a sit down at a four-star dive.

35

Sorry - We're Closed!

Nothing - but *nothing** - annoys me more than a business that keeps hours that seem ridiculously convenient for the owners, but insanely inconvenient for me.

*(Okay, lots of things to annoy me more, but right NOW, this is what I'm railing on.)

As a business owner, before you decide what your hours of operation are, please consider your core customer demographic. If you're selling yarn to octogenarians, then 9-5 is probably just fine. But if you're selling items that appeal to a wider audience, then you should, at the very least, consider expanding your hours.

How?

As always, I'm glad that you asked!

Many businesses will poll their customers, first and foremost.

When is the most convenient time for them to shop?

If you were open on weekends, or for longer periods of time, would they shop more often?

Are their friends or family *not* shopping there due to constraints imposed by your hours of operation?

Another tactic is when businesses tout new, expanded hours. This allows them a finite period of time to experience firsthand what they're missing. By expanding their hours on a test basis, they can assess how many phone calls, and how much foot traffic, they're receiving in relation to what they're already used to. And it may be an eye opener.

A word of caution: if you're going to try this, make *sure* that folks know that you are doing so *and* give it enough time to conclusively succeed or fail.

In the past, I have spoken with business owners who have done just this, only to find them saying something like, "Well, after two weeks, we didn't see enough traffic."

This is where the inner me wants to slap them upside the head and scream, "Well, Duh!"

Instead, I patiently explain that this probably is not a good benchmark to base such a profoundly important decision upon. And I'll be the first to admit that I might be wrong. But I don't believe that I am.

So as a small business owner, what can you do about this?

First and foremost, understand and recognize that you're not a superhero. You cannot work sixteen-hour days, seven days a week, without compromising on health, family, customer service, quality of work, faith, or a million other things.

I once came across a business concept that stated that underlings, at their peak, should only be expected to perform at 80-90% of your personal capabilities (when considering that they're doing a job that you've already mastered, or are more motivated to perform). Sometimes it's better. But don't expect that it will be. Hope for the best, but prepare for the worst.

Consider hiring part time help, or if there's a family member or friend you trust, consider offering them the work to cover the expanded hours. Trusting someone that you don't know, especially without supervision, can be a scary thing.

I didn't used to think so, until some of my employees did some unfathomably awful things. These things happened, and they sucked. And a lot of folks out there, no matter how nice they seem, can be prone to moments of weakness. I've seen good men do bad things, because no one was there to see them (or so they thought, until they saw the video).

My father always used to say, "Locks keep an honest man honest."

Even with those caveats, here's the reality: we eventually made more than enough money to cover those losses, because my company elected to continue trusting individuals, and offer expanded hours.

And you know what?

Ninety percent of those individuals are gems who would give you the shirts off of their backs. So there's far more good than bad out there. If there's an upside, it's that.

All in all, at least take a moment to contemplate how this section of the book might affect you.

Would expanded hours provide more business; more profit; more return on investment; a reduced burden rate?

If the answer to any of those questions is 'possibly', then you need to begin considering a plan of action. The customers are out there. But they can't shop if you won't take their money.

Turn Your Marketing Inward By Marketing Yourself, To Yourself

Sometimes, marketing can be as simple as being introspective about yourself, your physical selling, your business space, and your product or service. More often than not, humans tend to be creatures of habit, and averse to change.

Have you been doing things the same way, successfully, for 20 years?

That's great!

Now, what have you missed out on?

"But Heath!" you say, "Remember the adage: If it isn't broken, don't fix it!"

True enough. And I'm not saying that it's broken, necessarily.

Let me present it a different way:

Let's say that you have a lawnmower that you really love (and not in a Weird Uncle Pete way, either). You've mowed with it for 5 years, and it's cut your lawn without a hitch. But for 5 years, you did no preventive maintenance. So what you've missed is the fact that, over time, the lawnmower has lost productivity. It runs slower, and the blades are dull.

What does this mean, exactly?

It might mean that every time you mow your lawn, you're losing seven minutes of your life. It happens, and you don't even realize it.

Why?

It's simple: because mowing takes longer than it should, had preventive maintenance been done.

See the difference?

It isn't broken – it's doing what you need it to do. It's still mowing your lawn.

What it *isn't* doing, is functioning to its optimal level. And this is where the consideration of introspection comes in.

There are so many facets of your business that you can analyze, quantify, and attack. I recommend choosing one that seems most prominent, and working on it first. A good manager knows that you function this way, as do fighter pilots, interestingly enough. They compartmentalize problems, work in order of importance, and solve one before moving on to the next. And as a manager of 18 years and over 100 unique egos, collectively, I can tell you that it works. If you permit it to, that is.

So pick one issue and then follow it down the rabbit hole. Analyze your methods; consider time and motion management; concentrate on unanswered metrics and make them answerable; talk to your clients; consider the intuitiveness of your surroundings; think like a customer; think like a vendor; think like your thrifty cousin Myrtle.

Whatever it takes, throw preconceived notions out the window, and clear the slate of complacency in your mind. I guarantee you will be surprised at what you find. And moreover, the rewards that tweaking those things can bring.

Know Thy Customer - Specifically

Know your enemy - uh, customer!

There's always some sort of advertising available to you at any given moment, so long as you've got the cash to implement it. You know this.

What you may not realize is that you literally have to think like your customer before you can cater to their specific need(s) through the advertising medium(s). What this means is that for each diverse and targeted group, you will require an equally diverse and targeted advertising approach.

What's important to them?

What scares them?

What makes them happy?

What are they passionate about?

Answer these questions, and others like them before you consider where to put your advertising effort. The return on investment will be exponentially larger than if you just toss an ad out into the world and hope for something to happen.

Education Still Pays

Educate your *potential* customers to convert them into *actual* customers.

How?

As per usual, I'm ever so pleased that you inquired!

Let's say that what you offer is confusing, seems simple on the surface, or is just plain boring. I mean, let's face it, most products are not as exciting as a *Nintendo*, a crossbow, or a trampoline*. It's just a fact. So making your product or service look sexy can be a daunting task.

*(All three together, somehow, would be awesome, though!)

But it can be done.

The first thing you need to consider is what your product or service does, features, or offers that your clients would normally have no idea about. Let's take something mundane, and yet popular that I've already picked on once: Scented Candles. And a disclaimer here: I'm not belittling the plethoric world of these things. I know pretty much nothing about them. I just needed a rolling example.

Scented candles seem to be a product that people either think are flippin' amazing or – like me – are more forgettable than a seventh *Rocky* movie. So I'm a good choice to attempt to market to, because I truly believe I have zero need for these things.

What I actually do know is this: I know how to light one. I know sometimes they smell like something I want to eat. I know that they burn. I know that no matter how many you have burning in the bathroom at Thanksgiving dinner, someone's malodorous deuce will trump them all, every time. And there you have it.

So marketing to me would require you to convince me on some level that I can't live without these things.

Sound impossible?

Nope!

I'm going to show you my hand.

Ready?

Here's a list of my personal 'button issues' that might sway me to purchase one:

- o If they removed allergens, somehow.
- o If they created a pervasive and non-localized smell.
- o If they were made in a green way.
- o If their sale helped a cause I was passionate about.

That's about all I can think of that would make me reconsider these things. The biggest reasons would be #1 & #2. If they did that, I might now be a buyer.

But had I not just told you all of this, you would never know. So your journey starts with research. Finding out why folks buy them from you is a no-brainer. Finding folks who are indifferent to them and inquiring as to *why* they could give two figs about them will help you to tailor your marketing to a different crowd (and possibly make a sale when you prove that one of their hesitations is falsely realized).

It's difficult work. But if you take the time to glean this information, you can now sell to a whole new market via education (remember education – the topic of this section?) Present everyone who will listen with educational facts, packaged in short, succinct bursts. And when you run out, feel free to go cyclical with it. Perhaps you could also develop a list of perceived falsehoods about the product.

"No, they will not make you sterile, get you laid, or cause blindness in wombats. Those are all myths!"

Whatever your product might be, educating your consumers, especially the potential ones, is a great way to turn a negative into a positive. But you *must* take the time to get inside the heads of your non-customers to do this to its most effective end.

Criticism: When It Comes Knocking, Let It In, And Make It Feel At Home

Criticism.

Now, before we go any further, how many of you just cringed a little?

It's all right. That's natural. We as human beings are naturally averse to criticism. And that's okay, so long as you can break yourself of that habit.

Why would you want to?

Criticism is a tool, and not - in point of fact - a thing to be reviled.

You will never please everyone all of the time. It's an impossibility. Striving to, on the other hand, is something that you as business owners should always put at the forefront of your daily lives.

With criticism, the first truth you have to accept is that it comes in two forms:

40

Angry criticism: Jack-wagons who like to yell about how awful something was, instead of being rational.

Constructive criticism: When people are levelheaded, and genuinely concerned with making a difference.

Both are relevant, and both - it's sad to admit - are important.

Criticism is your customer's way of telling you that something needs fixing. How you respond to it could make or break your business. Remember the old adage:

"The customer is always right!"

We all know that isn't *completely* true. What we have to remember, then, is this:

"The customer always thinks that they're right."

And sometimes, though it may pain you, you have to play along with that little farce.

There was a statement that I once read (I don't specifically recall where, now) that cited something that has always stuck with me:

"For every person that complains about something, there were ten who did not."

So when someone complains, consider it as coming from eleven people. This, I've found, is extremely prescient insight into the minds of consumers.

Recently, a good friend of mine (who is a foodie and chef-type) was upset about the fate of a genuinely constructive post that he had placed on a moderately priced, higher-end restaurant's *Facebook* page.

Their response?

They simply deleted it. That was it. No public or private response. Nope. Deletion of the post, for them, 'solved' the problem.

Here was what he posted to his friends in the aftermath, just to prove my point further:

"Shame, too. I have had very good pizza there every other time we were there. I have told tons of friends about the place. And you know what they say about dissatisfied customers."

Guess where he and his circle of 350+ friends will no longer be going? How much money did that establishment just lose with that one single, mouse click?

I personally ran into this sort of situation on one of the *Facebook* pages that I admin for, last year. I announced that I would be doing a book signing, and that a portion of the proceeds from book sales would be going to *The Salvation Army*.

Within an hour or so, a response was posted. It read:

"Are you aware that The Salvation Army *doesn't support same-sex relationships?"*

Actually, I wasn't. But that also hadn't been among my considerations when choosing a charitable organization to allocate funds to.

My first response was, I'm guessing, very unlike what yours might have been. And this is only because I've trained myself to think differently over many years. I took a step back and analyzed the situation.

Why was this post here, of all places?

What was this person attempting to gain?

Here's what I guessed: She had had a bad experience with *The Salvation Army* in the past, and - right or wrong - this was her way of retaliating.

Instead of deleting it, I addressed it cordially. I didn't call her names. I didn't belittle her right to post such a thing. I just responded honestly and openly in a friendly manner.

Then, I went further. I sent her a private message inquiring what her negative experience had been, and why she had felt compelled to post this.

Want to know what happened?

I'll just assume you said, "Yes."

We had a very long, grown-up conversation about the whole thing, and parted as respected equals. I showed her that her concerns important enough not to be ignored, and even went so far as to take the time to understand them. Not only did I save a relationship I didn't even know I had (she was subscribed to the page, but I didn't bring her there personally), I made a friend and salvaged a potential client or conduit for clients down the road.

All of this happened, because I didn't just dismiss her criticism.

And you shouldn't either. No matter how insane the criticism might seem on the surface, listen to it. Ask questions. And even if you don't agree with the viewpoint of the harbinger of this ill portent, at least gain their perspective to assist you in the future when considering things said and done.

Above all, never, never, NEVER (there's those pesky caps again) ignore criticism or – worse – dismiss it. You're doing the bringer a disservice, and you're doing yourself an even more egregious one.

Networking: It Isn't All About You

Networking: you've all heard the word. You probably also have a fairly good idea of what it entails. For those of you who believe it is 'getting yourself out there' (virtually or physically), you're partially right. However, a big part of networking is being able to do it correctly, to do it well, and more to the point, successfully.

Here's what I mean:

Let's start in meat-space (i.e. – 'real world interaction'). If you intend upon going to a networking function with the notion of letting everyone there know how amazing your business is, you've already failed. Do yourself a favor and stay home.

For those of you nodding in agreement right now, pat yourself on the back. You get it. For those of you who think I'm insane and have just negated the entire desired result, that's all right as well. I'll do my best to make you a convert before this section is over.

Networking is 90% listening, and 10% marketing. What this means is that many of the individuals with whom you interact will want to do exactly what I have just advised you not to do.

And that's okay!

You're not really there for them to market to you. You didn't leave the comforts of your home thinking only, "Boy! I hope someone sells me that home facial waxing kit that they're so passionate about!"

Think about that truth as I continue this crazy section.

Most folks who attend these events are amateurs in the realm of networking. They see it as an opportunity to preach to a room full of strangers who simply *must* know about the *ColonBlaster 7000* system that they're selling.

And they're wrong.

These folks are all sharks in a proverbial tank. Every one of them is looking for prey, not looking to be eaten. And as such, they will attempt myriad tactics to feed. Their inexperience, however, will most likely end up making them either food or – at the very best – remoras; hangers-on to the larger whole.

So how does one work this situation to their advantage?

Here's what I do, right or wrong. I know my product. I am passionate about my product. I am passionate about what I can do for these people, and I consider every one of them a potential customer, whether they realize that they require my services or not. My job is to make this revelation visible to them and, if I don't or can't, to understand why I didn't.

43

Now some of these folks will be so prophet-ous about their product or service that they will either (intentionally or unintentionally) tune out all comers. Be polite, but don't get stuck with these folks. Cut your losses and move on. But before you do, make damn sure that you're correct about your sizing up of them. If you're not 100% sure, hang on a little longer.

Others will corner you and prattle on and on about their product. This is okay, so long as you're getting something out of it. To do so, consider leading questions that will still keep them talking about their offering, but also have relevance to what you're bringing to the table. In my case, if someone is lauding the benefits of their – let's say, scented candles (something I will never buy – sorry gang) – I could have them consider and describe their distribution channels. If I can move the conversation in a direction that makes them realize that they could do more business with, let's say, a web site, I have now made the conversation bilateral, rather than unilateral.

In fact, if I can ask the right questions, in the right order, 'disguising' them as questions to their benefit, I can eventually move the conversational poles from their advantage to mine. It's a subtle shift that takes time, energy, and effort. But it can be done.

And please: don't think I'm some jerk. I'm really not. If I'm interested in your product I will, in fact, be curious about it for the product's sake - truly. But more often than not, I won't be.

So I'll be trying to size you up as a potential client. To keep you invested, I might drop conversation starters about things that might interest you. There are two gifts that I'd like to believe that I possess: I can tell an interesting story, and I have some interesting experiences. Both are gifts that I treasure. I understand that these are not something that everyone has.

"That's great, you Napoleonic maniac," you might be saying. "That's *you*. So where does that leave *me*?"

You just have to be hyper-introspective about what you can bring to the table, and then hone your skills. Stories can be as simple as fondly remembering the time your brother was three, and tried to flush a stuffed beaver down the toilet, flooding the bathroom because he thought it wanted to swim*. We've all experienced goofy stuff like this, so use things like that in your conversational arsenal whenever appropriate. Remember: funny never equals boring.

(That's a true story, by the way. Sorry for outing you, Nick.)

Another important aspect of networking in real life is being able to think on your feet. You need to be able to read the other listener(s) 'tells' as to when they're either enthralled, or thinking about how awesome that pot roast was last night. This is important because it's the tipping point. If it tips the wrong way, that's your cue to move on. And try not to spend too much time with any one individual. It is, after all, networking. You're not choosing a mate for life. You owe these folks nothing more than common courtesy. And I would strongly suggest that you be liberal with that. They're all just people like you, with feelings, needs, and desires.

An additional idea that you can employ to your advantage is to strategically attend functions where your current or former clients are - especially if you've wowed them. If you're lucky, they'll gush about you, and send business your way without you having to take the initiative. This is also a positive, in that you don't have to gear up to talk about your thing – these potential customers are seeking you out, already primed.

I could go on and on (just ask my wife). But you get the idea.

Networking = Good
Aimless chatter = Bad
Being buttonholed = Very bad.

Now, let's turn the thought process to Virtual Space. For me, networking in Virtual Space was something that I accidentally learned in my mid- to late-teens. Back then, we still had computers (crazy, I know, but true, nonetheless). Only, instead of all the things that you're probably familiar with, we had the *Galacticomm BBS, TelNet, MajorNET,* Door Games and *WinSOCK*'s. If you don't know what I'm talking about then – congratulations – you're probably good at sports. For those of us that typically weren't, we had our computers.

The environments we inhabited were primitive in comparison to today's standards. It was a pre-GUI, *DOS*-based nightmare to the outside observer. To us, it was a virtual home whose 'rooms' and 'spaces' we could 'see' in our mind's eye. And if we had a modem (can I get a shout out for a 1200 baud *Hayes*, here?) we could pay monthly 'credit' fees to be allowed to participate on a Bulletin Board System. These were real-time community systems, similar to *Facebook* today, but not even remotely as robust. They afforded folks a chance to get to know one another in a backward manner. You could only see what was inside of someone, long before you met them.

What I quickly learned was that I was fairly good at networking, even though I had no idea that what I was doing back then had an official name.

In school I was bullied, I had few friends, and girls thought as much of me as they did their father's thermal hunting socks.

By the time I made it online I had a solid knowledge of all things trivial, I was funny, and I was a good listener who – I was told – gave sage advice. I met people virtually. Their first impressions of me were far more genuine than they ever could have been in real life meat-space, and vice-versa. As such, my list of virtual friends grew. Many of them are still my very close and dear friends today, both in the real world, and on *Facebook*. I even married one, and we've spent the past seventeen years completely mental for one another.

In retrospect, I took all of those things that I had inadvertently learned all those years ago, and put them into practice when beginning my new business endeavor. I had already secured my friends, past and present, but in order to market my business appropriately, I had to branch out into new territory.

I chose to do this by joining, and participating on, *Facebook* - a lot. I participated in friends of friend's inquiries in a helpful way. I joined groups that I felt were of interest to me, and participated in those. And I didn't just participate – I crafted. I made a conscious effort to make the entries short, poignant, relevant, and most of all funny where appropriate.

After a couple of weeks, I started receiving messages from friends. Some of which said something akin to, "So and so is a friend of mine and they really like what you have to say. Would it be weird if they friended you?"

As a former geek (we actually coined the term for ourselves in the eighties, in case you were wondering where it came from – and we're damn proud of it) this was something I had already done in past decades (i.e. - meet new people who just 'showed up' to the live TeleConference feed and dive right in). So for me, it made no difference at all. Suddenly, I was making new connections. It was taking me back in time. I was a social chameleon once again, and I loved the satisfaction of every new connection, as I learned new things about new people and made new friends. Trust me – you can never have too many friends. And mine are awesome.

As time went on, and more and more folks seemed to tune in to what I was up to, I elected to begin giving them a social outlet for specific needs to be met. I developed groups on *Facebook* that I could intelligently weigh in on, while adding to my circle of friends and acquaintances. This took (and still takes) an immense amount of time and effort on my part. The perpetual reward is folks seeking me out for answers to all sorts of things – odd or otherwise. And I am only too happy to help. Without anyone realizing it, I had soft-sold them on myself. I didn't push my business on them. I just assisted them with their issues, rather than prattling on about how great my business is. I had networked. And I was helping them –

something I truly love to do. Many of them are my customers now.

Whatever the means to the end for you, keep all of these thoughts in mind. Cater to the needs of others, and cultivate new relationships. Help new people wherever and whenever you may. They will be more inclined to seek you out, and hopefully want to know more about you (and your product).

And for Heaven's sake, be *ready* for this!

Not knowing your product, in and out, and not being passionate about it, are major turn offs.

Who wants to buy stuff from you that even *you're* indifferent about?

So get yourself out there!

Learn from your mistakes and celebrate your victories. And if you need me, I'm always here for you. For networking purposes, of course, but also because I genuinely like to see everyone succeed. And I never turn down the opportunity to make a new friend.

Commit Random Acts Of Gratitude

'Thank you'.

Just two simple words; two syllables. It takes a microsecond to speak them. Yet in this day and age, it is a term which often goes unused; is underused; or is used incorrectly or disingenuously. Let's take a moment to re-kindle our recognition of the profound usefulness of this term.

Let's begin at the beginning. How many times have you heard someone say, "Thanks," in passing, and considered whether it was due to rote programming, or whether it was the result of a sincere appreciation of the act leading to the utterance?

While good manners are, in fact, important (and I'm looking at you, here, Weird Uncle Pete), it is equally important that the manners utilized are so performed with the purest intent.

Every day at work (i.e. - 'my day job') I see volumes of quotation requests come across my desk. Additionally, I see a similar volume of purchase orders from clients as well. And I'm betting that many of you during your business day have a similar experience that you can equate to this.

At their core, these quotations and orders are tacit, physical embodiments of the faith and trust we have earned from our clients or, on occasion, a new opportunity to do so. The normal thing to do would be to process them as required, and then move on to something else. And this would be 95% correct.

But what if you took a step back, and considered what each of those documents *really* meant. Each quotation request is an opportunity, afforded to you or your company. Each purchase order is a financial boost provided by a client, and a vote of confidence in your skills or product.

Now imagine your life, and your employee's and co-worker's lives, if those quotations and purchase orders suddenly ceased to exist.

If you just heard your brain go *PLINK,* then you're in the Zen zone for this segment. If you didn't, then re-read the last paragraph, and arrive at this point anew. Go ahead. I don't mind waiting.

47

...

All set?

If not, then lie to me. We haven't got *all* day.

Oftentimes, I keep a close eye on who's sending me what, and when. If I see a heavy flow all of the sudden from a client that I don't normally see it from, I assess the situation. I often take a few minutes to craft a sincere, appreciative 'thank you' e-mail (calls are nice, but they can't be dealt with at your customer's discretion, and so I avoid them). It might read something like this:

">Dude/Dudette's Name Here<:

Good morning/afternoon! I just wanted to take a moment to personally thank for all of the opportunities to quote that you have recently sent. We're truly honored that you have allowed us the opportunity to serve your needs, and we hope that you will continue to place your trust in us as new projects arise. We appreciate everything that you do for us, and should there be anything that I may do further, please don't hesitate to call me personally. Thank you, again, for your continued faith and patronage."

To be fair, they're usually a substantial bit better than this, as they're more specific - I target certain key words that are customer and buyer specific, so the above example looks a bit droll. Notice what I did, though: I took the time to plant suggestions in their head by using words like *'faith'* and *'trust'*, a phrase like *'serve your needs'*, and most important of all *'appreciate'*. When I am done crafting such a letter, I make sure it reads as 100% sincere, because it's meant to be. If it comes off as crass or disingenuous, or - worse - forced, then it has a negative effect. We don't want any of that. And, a letter such as this is a far cry from dashing off a note that says, *'Thanks for the quotes!'* isn't it?

Which would *you* rather receive?

Which would garner your genuine attention?

Gratitude is free. To my surprise, over the years, I have noticed that when I send these, that I often receive unasked-for reciprocal praise. This means that I not only got through to the customer, it also means that I have a soft spot in their psyche that another vendor may not.

And I don't stop at just customers when it comes to parceling out gratitude. When a vendor comes through for me in a big way, I personally write a thank-you. This way, they know their work was not only noticed (by the guy at the top, no less) but *appreciated*. And trust me when I say that they're far more likely to do that sort of thing again in the future for you, versus those other guys and gals who ride them hard and never thank them.

It's true. I've proven it, time and time again.

Not good at writing letters?

That's all right. Just be honest and open as you craft. Use a spell-checker if you have access to one. If you're *really* lousy at composing, develop a few manipulate-able letters that can be tailored later.

Finally, it's always a good idea to let a third party read it. This might seem absurd, but it affords an opportunity to assess the potential impact of the letter, potential problems in the message, or emotions that might be coming through the wrong way. It never hurts to put a second set of eyes on anything.

In closing, I want to say 'thank you' to you. Without you, I would have no audience. Without your feedback, I would not feel compelled to continue writing.

Thank you, most sincerely.

Pride: A Five-Letter Word That Can Win Or Lose Customers, As Well As The Respect Of Your Peers

Let's face it: we're all human. More specifically, I assume that we all are, because aliens are really good at hiding, and Sasquatches don't write newspaper columns too often. Then, there's Weird Uncle Pete who may very well fall into a category all his own. But, for the most part: human.

As humans, we all have pride hardwired into our psyche. Pride is so engrained in us that the Catholic Church has gone out of their way to let us know that it's on the seven most-unwanted list. And it's a natural response. When we do something well, we're proud of our efforts. This is fine, to a degree. This is healthy, so long as you don't go all Jim Jones about it and start offering free *Kool-Aid*. It's when we allow pride to begin clouding (or worse, precluding) rational thought, that we start to run into some trouble.

Pride can be a fickle thing. It can make us say and do things that our rational mind knows to be wrong, or at the very least not the best idea in the world. This is where we need to take a step back, assess ourselves, and be prepared to acknowledge that - again - we're human.

In business, the adage of *'Pride goeth before the fall'* is all too true. I have personally been a victim of this vice from time to time. In hindsight, the only one that I hurt was myself.

In fact, I let it get in the way of a customer interaction, just the other day. I allowed my pride to immediately jump to the conclusion that my customer was wrong - and that I was right - based on my wealth of computer knowledge in relation to her veritable lack of it.

Do you want to know what happened?

It turned out that we were both wrong.

She was experiencing a two-fold problem. First, her version of *Internet Explorer* was bringing up a cached version of one of the web sites that we had written for her. Second, *Bing* was doing some stupid things I didn't even know could happen.

In the end, I took a step back, listened, had her show me what she was experiencing, and we devised a solution (clear the cache, and make one minor tweak to allow *Bing* not to do stupid things to us anymore.)

Had I not done this, and had I instead let pride take the reins, I may have lost a customer, and their respect for me as well.

How awful and stupid would that have been?

Allowing yourself to possess a 'pride override' switch is a learned trait. My first piece of advice is to assume that you are, in fact, wrong. No matter how much you know that you're right, because you're nearly deified in your own mind. Humble yourself to a basic level, and work the issue at hand like a geometry proof. Take the issue step by step and empirically prove that you are as right as you believe yourself to be.

Know what will happen?

You'll find the problem with a level head, and retain your good standing with the public at large. Or in the best-case scenario, you'll be able to walk the other individual(s) through why you're right, proving to them in a kind and gentle way that they've made an error.

If it goes the second way, I'd also highly recommend playing it down. *Waaaaay* down. I like to make folks feel more comfortable about their misconceptions or errant ways by giving the, '*Aw, shucks. This sort of stuff happens all the time. If this is the worst thing that happens today, it'll still be a great day*' speech - that sort of thing. Because their pride might be damaged at just that moment, and an inferiority complex brought on by your smug derision probably isn't going to gain you any brownie points.

This concept also works well with employee interactions. When I was a young manager (read: really, abysmally, horribly bad at managing) I would get visibly upset about situations. I learned fast that I was a moron.

When you approach a situation with delicacy and tact, your employees, too, feel better about themselves, and are more open to gentle coaxing in the form of friendly advice on how not to make the same mistake. I also take the time to recall that I'm human, and make mistakes as well.

I sometimes take this a step further by attempting to relay a similar story to their plight, should I have one.

"Heck, last week I did so-and-so, so compared to that, this is nothing."

It humanizes you as a manager, and levels the mental playing field by removing the 'us versus them' wall that often exists between employers and employees. Now we have something in common, and I seem to understand their plight because – well - we do, and I have.

So in the words of Glen Campbell, "Try a little kindness." Don't be glib, prideful, or angry when something goes wrong. Treat the situation as you would wish to be treated, were the roles reversed. I guarantee your street cred will soar, and respect will follow closely behind in the majority of cases.

Channel Your Grandmother - Not Hitler
Be friendly!

It seems like a simple enough concept, doesn't it?

But how often do your friends and relatives regale you with a story that goes something like this:

"I can't believe how friendly and accommodating this company was! They listened to everything I had to say, and made me feel special."

To be fair, it *does* happen. But not nearly as often as you hear something like this:

"The guy was a total jerk! I stood there for twenty minutes, he got my order wrong, I couldn't understand a word he said, he smelled like a rutting musk ox, and he slouched on the counter. Then his thirty-five piercings got caught in his vest and he kept dropping f-bombs, not even looking at me – like I wasn't even there!"

How many times a week do you see or hear rants of *this* sort?

If you're like most folks, then it amounts to more times than is healthy for your blood pressure.

Your interactive customer experience begins the moment that you begin communicating – verbally *or* physically – with a representative of the company. And if you don't think this moment is important, and that I'm stating what should be the obvious, then come here so I can have Weird Uncle Pete poke you in the eye with something pointy, because you're wrong *and* stupid.

That's right: I went there.

Now for those of you sensible folks (and hopefully those of you now mortally a'feared of being poked in the eye by some poodle-infatuated lunatic that you've never met): listen up.

Everything about your person, from the time you set eyes upon the customer until the time they are safely out the door, is important. It is *vastly* important. Everything from your body language to your tone of voice can make a customer feel loved and welcomed. Or conversely, it can make them feel spurned like a pariah in a new and as-yet-undiscovered tenth circle of Hell. It's really all up to you.

Let's begin at the beginning.

If you're on the phone with a client or customer, then you're off the hook for the appearance portion. Your voice, however, needs to clearly convey the following things:

- I'm attentive
- I'm easy to understand
- I'm friendly
- I'm smiling
- I know your time is valuable
- I'll get you to your desired end, in one way or another
- Let me worry for you!
- I have nothing more to do at this precise moment than to make your life better

If your voice isn't conveying all of these things, then congratulations to your competition - they just scored a point against you. At the machine shop that I run (i.e. – 'my day job'), we have a mandatory way of answering the phone. It's something we pound into each other's heads.

Why?

In our industry, 90% of the phone calls that we make are not received with any or all of the above criteria. And frankly, we like it that way.

Again: why?

Because it means we're in a minority. And as such, we've developed a clear advantage.

Even after the phone is answered, we *ask* permission of the caller to remind them that they're in control: if they could hold, if they would care to speak to the person, or if leaving a message is more convenient, etc. We always make the options theirs to wield as they see fit. Telephonic Dictatorialism isn't even in our lexicon (and it might not even be a real thing, but it sounds sort of cool).

Another thing that sets us apart is the fact that we intentionally don't have voice mail. We hop-to and find the person you want to talk to, via two-way radio, and get them on the phone ASAP.

Why?

Because we know that our client's time is valuable, and voice mail (in our humble opinion) is most often counter-productive in our industry. I often find that my customer's time is of the essence, when it comes to doling out projects. And if I'm there to answer a customer's inquiry personally, while they reach a voice mailbox at my competition (who may call them back or may be in Tahiti for all they know), I find that they start calling me first.

It's actually a proven fact.

Do you know how I know this?

Because my customers have actually gone out of their way to tell me how awesome we are at interpersonal communication. Honest to God. It's true.

When customers (potential or otherwise) arrive at our shop, we greet them with a smile. We shake hands. We offer beverages and a seat. We make and hold eye contact. We make them feel like they've just walked into their Grandmother's kitchen, and they're the only central focus of our world at the moment. And we treat them as such until the time they leave.

Know what else?

We do the same for vendors and everyone else. It's amazing what a little friendliness, kindness, respect, and a smile can bring about. Seriously – you'd be amazed.

For example: our UPS guy likes to use our clean bathroom, he knows who we all are by name, we let him store his ice cream novelties in our freezer in the summer months. For all of this feeling of home, he will wait for packages that aren't quite ready, or even come back around to our place after another part of his run. Neither of which he is obligated to do, and both of which, in fact, effect his day negatively.

One of our steel delivery drivers uses our microwave to heat his lunch up. In exchange, he helps us unload his truck, and will even go out of his way to make us a priority when we desperately need it. Sometimes, he even brings us some of his amazing, homemade cookies.

Neither of these fellows has to do these things. They choose to do so because we treat them very well, and this is how they feel compelled to reciprocate.

So if you're not doing all of these things then please – for your own sake – do! And more importantly, make sure that your employees do as well! If they're prone to profanity, poor body language, mumbling, or any other negative habits then, for goodness sake, correct them.

Want to take it a step further?

Call the office or shop at random, and experience first-hand how the phone is answered when you're not there.

Was it quickly answered?

Was the receiver of the call friendly?

Could you understand them, or were they giving John Moschitta a run for his title?

Did their voice evoke a mental picture of someone smiling, or a Goth kid wallowing in a vortex of apathy?

You can also expound on this idea with the 'secret shopper' concept. Have someone you know, but your employees do not, come to the store. In the aftermath, ask them to critique their experience. I can almost guarantee that there's something happening that you won't like.

And that's okay!

It's not like your employees are out to screw you (well, not necessarily). Perhaps it's simply a case of them not having been taught what is correct, or expected of them. If they're failing, look to yourself as a manager and proprietor for fault first - because it's your gig, not theirs. Blame, unfortunately, begins with leadership. Accept that fact, and you're on the road to rectification.

Use these tools & tactics and I believe - no, scratch that - I *promise* that you will see a difference in your customer's attitude.

And if you choose not to do so?

That's fine, too. But don't say that I didn't warn you.

F.T.L.: Your Million Dollar Nemesis

It has often been said that everyone, at one point in time in their life, has at least one million-dollar idea.

So if that's true, then why aren't we all millionaires?

The answer is a little (but important) acronym that I guarantee you've faced down and lost the battle to at least once before: F.T.L.

What is F.T.L.?

It's a business acronym that stands for (F)ailure (T)o (L)aunch.

We all have good ideas. Some correspond to our everyday lives, while others are focused on our businesses. Whatever these ideas may be, the greatest disservice one can do to oneself – or to one's business – is to leave those great ideas to languish in a void of eternal purgation.

So how does this avoidance policy work?

It's as simple as capturing the idea, developing a timeframe around it, and then following through with that rollout timeframe via development of the idea to a point where it fits comfortably within your day-to-day life, or business model.

Sounds a little complex, doesn't it?

Well it is, and it isn't.

The problem usually centers on deciding if it is an idea that needs to be implemented now, in the near future, in the distant future, or when time permits. Once that's been decided, it's a good idea to develop a reminder system for yourself, be they sticky notes on your refrigerator, or the use of *Outlook,* or other like-minded software, to keep hounding you. Whatever works for you is fine. The point is that you don't want to forget these ideas, because often, when you remember them, it's because something negative has happened and you recall how you once considered a potential solution to that situation.

So don't fall into the F.T.L. trap!

Document, remind, develop, timeline, streamline, and – most importantly – implement your way to success, one idea at a time.

Some Very Specific, General Information

Before I get into this, lest anyone question my position or outlook, let's just clear the air.

>Ahem<

War is Hell. It is rarely pure or just. Yet the men and women who are sent to fight it hold true to their vow, and their desire to believe in the individuals moving the pieces, that some greater good may come from their actions. Whether the motive proves just or no, their efforts and commitment are what need to be recollected. If we all did our duty as committed citizens, as they do as soldiers, then this country would be far more deserving of their actions and their sacrifice.

There. Now you know where I stand*. Now we'll get to the point of this section.

*(And thank you, to any veterans who might be reading this. I appreciate the heck out of you.)

Battlefield mentality + your business = phenomenal success

"Heath, you dipstick," I hear you thinking. "Have you gone off your nut?" Nope! Here's what I mean:

In the military, there exists a clear, structured chain of command. Why?

The simple answer is that very rarely will two people agree on much of anything. So someone must be in charge, to be the ultimate decision maker for the group. If they're good at it, they can convince an entire platoon that they're all super heroes, and can walk through all of that shrapnel flying at them with nothing but success.

If, on the other hand, they're not so good at it, they end up with all those folks depending on them being killed - or worse for them - a group of under-confident individuals who might seriously consider 'accidentally' shooting them in the butt.

I'm exaggerating to some degree, but here's where I'm going with this. When you began your business, you more than likely also became the General. You might not realize that that's the role you're playing, but it's true.

Have you considered this before?

If not, then do it – R-I-G-H-T N-O-W (there are our friends the caps again – and they even brought hyphens along for the party!)

Being the General means making good decisions, being a leader who is looked up to, and a leader whose army will follow them through Hell and back. Your army is your staff. If that description doesn't sound like them, then you're doing it wrong.

I'll make an example of myself, not to self-aggrandize, but to give you an idea of the responsibility that I am called upon to wield successfully (with commensurate consequences, should I not meet certain benchmarks or criteria) each and every day, and how I do it successfully.

At my day job, I am an Operations Manager for a contract machine shop. The company employs 30 individuals, male and female, ranging in age from nineteen to sixty-five. I am responsible for running the day-to-day operations of the business, with the exception of hiring, and firing, unless the owner is away (which he often is).

I have hired people, and I have fired people - both are awkward, and not things that I particularly enjoy.

How does my employer rate my performance?

During each of my employee's annual reviews, he inquires about my specific performance in interacting with them. Then, during *my* performance review, he outlines shortcomings, and strengths that have been uncovered during those sessions. I never get to know who said what.

As hard as this might seem to take, this makes me a better manager. The criticism he's providing is fuel to drive me to *be* a better manager.

I have been in this position for nigh on twenty years. When I began, I wielded zero respect on the shop floor. Truth be told, I was a lousy manager – beyond lousy. I don't even think, 'God-awful' would be undeserved, when it comes to describing my abilities and performance.

But I was a lousy manager who wanted to better himself. So I learned, I read, I watched, and I walked softly. Over the years, I have earned the respect of the vast majority of my employees. Every day, I am forced to earn it all over again, lest I lose it, or permit it to wane.

To earn that respect, I had to be a good General. I had to listen to the troop's ideas, comments, complaints, and thoughts. Then, I had to act in the best interests of the company. My decisions, therefore, could make or break the company in subtle ways – or profound ones – at any given moment.

I could blow up on an employee, and be a jerk to him or her, or I could take them aside, listen to their grievances, offer suggestions, or fix the problems.

I could make poor decisions without a second thought, or I could walk the employee through my thought process, ask for their thoughts on the matter, and show them that the decision I reached was well reasoned – and often reliant upon their specific expertise.

I could talk behind the backs of my employees or I could build them up to others.

I could offer them sincere credit for their contributions, or I could claim them for my own.

It was once explained to me that respect is akin to currency in a bank account. For every positive act of praise, you are making a 'deposit' in that account. For every negative reprimand, you are making a withdrawal.

What's the point?

If you make more withdrawals than deposits, your account no longer remains solvent. And no one wants to be destitute. So I take the time to do things, such as not only showing respect and reverence for a good idea. Often, I even tell others within the company about the great idea that so-and-so had.

And when I do have to reprimand them?

They take it in stride. I make sure that we understand one another, and then it's behind us – no grudges, no pettiness.

When I make a mistake I own up to it without hesitation. I have no qualms about letting my employees know that I have made an error. I will often take it a step further, discussing it with my subordinates to gain their perspective on how I could have done something different. This not only 'humanizes' me to the employee, it shows that even I need their help for things to run properly because – well – I do. Each of us plays a role in making the whole function smoothly and, more importantly, properly.

Without them, I wouldn't have a company to manage. I wouldn't have a paycheck, and I'm not ashamed to admit that to them.

In your role as the General, you need to do all of these things.

Why?

Because if you do, you will have a staff that you can address, and they will hear you. You may ask them to work late, come in on a Sunday, or do something difficult, and they will do so, out of the deference that you will have earned. You can make reasonable demands, and decisions they may not always agree with. As a good General, you will have earned the right to do so.

Anyone can be labeled a 'manager'. Only an elite few can actually measure up to the moniker. With every passing day, I strive to achieve that elite-ness. I may never reach it, but that doesn't prevent me from trying, just the same. I often fail, but learning from those failures makes me stronger. And openly sharing my failures eliminates the 'us versus them' mentality in the workplace, and develops a group-mind mentality to problem solving.

Consider all of this the next time that you interact with an employee. Be a kind, loving, flexible, gentle, approachable, stern (when necessary), appreciative, cognizant General – and your troops will follow your command, even if they don't understand the larger picture, or agree with you. Once you've earned that right, operating your business becomes a whole lot easier, and a lot less combative.

57

Work *On* Your Business, Not *In* It

Years ago, I learned a business principle that seemed - well - stupid. Oh, how times have changed, and how much I've grown. I was presented with an adage:

"Work on the business, not in the business."

To me, this seemed counter-intuitive: wasn't a person in business to make money by - well - running it and working to make a profit?

The answer is far more complex than you might imagine. Further, it can - and does - pertain not only to small, medium, and large businesses, but cottage businesses as well.

So what does this mean?

In a nutshell we, as business owners, spend a ton of time making our business go. We make the product or perform the service that is at the core of the business model.

In smaller businesses, we are often compelled to act as bookkeeper, salesperson, vendor, buyer, manager, and a number of other positions simultaneously because, without these tasks being performed by an unpaid individual (i.e. - you) the business just isn't strong enough to function in this infant state.

As the business grows, one needs to become more aware of when to do something oneself, or when to delegate a task. This frees up time to perform higher functions within the business, or functions that you are more capable of performing than a delegate would be. For most, delegation will be one of the toughest decisions that you will ever make as a business owner. Not making the decision to do so, however, can be a one-way ticket to stunting your business growth. Over time, delegation becomes more and more important. For the most part, you are not an accountant (unless you actually are, then please pretend that I said some other business-y position that you aren't), nor are you likely a salesperson, a techie, a manager, an HR genius, and on and on. Over time, it makes more sense to delegate these tasks to paid professionals, or new hires who have the requisite capabilities, so that you can work on growing the business.

Also, when delegation occurs, prepare for disappointment. The reality is that almost no one will do the job 100% as you would. I'd also bank on the fact that no one else will be 100% as efficient as you.

This is, in fact, normal - don't freak out!

In my experience, I have been advised that you may expect a 70-90% rate of efficiency when delegating, versus performing a task yourself. While I think 70% is a bit on the lackluster side, I have come to comprehend this 'loss of core competency' phenomena. Over time, I have become far more comfortable with expecting – and dealing - with it.

As the business grows, and you get older (and you will get older), there comes a time where the business will stagnate. This is fine, if this is in the plan. If not, then one of the hats on your head needs to come off, and be put upon someone else's noggin. It's the only sane way to free up time, and in the end, if you've grown the business to its fullest, you will be doing nothing but reviewing content provided by delegates, and making steering decisions for the future of the venture.

Not ready for that?

That's all right too!

Grow your business as much or as little as you like. It's a good idea to have some semblance of an idea in place as to how large you are willing to get. Bear in mind, however, that with larger size, comes larger rewards. It may sound like it will suck the life right out of you, but it can be a very rewarding time in the life cycle of the enterprise. It's a time when you get to do all of the 'fun' things that you love, while benefitting financially. Plus, you receive additional 'you' time from all of the hard work and effort that has brought you as far as you've come. The delegates are paid to handle the day-to-day work. You're just there to make sure that it's done to your standards and expectations (and those that your customers have come to expect).

So focus on a goal of working on the business - not in it. Enjoy the sliding scale of reward that comes with a job well done, and a life well lived. After all: you can't take it with you. And you never know when your time card will get that final punch.

Everything Is Negotiable

No, you did not read that wrong.

When I was taking classes for my real estate salesperson's licensure, the teacher once said, "Everything is negotiable."

GUERRILLA BUSINESS ♦ HEATH D. ALBERTS

Someone questioned how that was possible, and he gave this example:

Potential Buyer: "Will you give me the house for free?"

Salesperson: "No."

"There," he decreed, "we've just negotiated."

It sounds sort of dumb, but he was dead-on correct. Just because negotiation ends in a stalemate, doesn't negate the fact that it has, in fact, occurred.

I know a fellow who made it one of his missions in life to negotiate everything. And folks, I mean literally *everything*. This fellow would negotiate with *Girl Scouts* for cookie discounts. Well, all right, that's probably a lie. But it's a lie that gets my point across.

We, as individuals, are often in one of three camps:

- Those who are unafraid to negotiate
- Those who are scared to death of conflict, and who will not negotiate
- Those who don't consider negotiation as a viable option

If you're in camp one, then you can probably just skim to the next segment (though, there might be something here for you, just the same.)

If you're in camp two, then you really need to do your best to get over that anxiety that comes with negotiation in the first place. I know, it's tough. But it's in your best interests.

If you're in the third camp, then listen closely as I say (well, type, technically) again: everything is negotiable.

Consider every facet of your business that falls outside the scope of your entire, direct control. Those are defined, in this case, as 'things'. Therefore, they are 'negotiable'.

I'm going to get a bit long-winded in a moment, because I really, really want to open your mind to the possibilities that solid negotiation brings. Some examples (read: a ton of examples) are:

- Talking to your bank about waiving those pesky fees
- Talking with your credit card provider about lowering those pesky interest rates
- Attempting one-time price adjustments on procured items
- Seeking overstock, 'scratch and dent', and 'closeout' items, and then negotiating the price downward
- Are discounts available from vendors if you pay within, say, ten days of receiving a bill? If not, would they be willing to accommodate

that?
- Are discounts available if you pay for a service a year in advance? (i.e. – alarm monitoring)
- Is there a corporate 'version' of your office supply provider, where additional savings may be had?
- Will your oft-used vendor agree to discounts on commonly purchased items?
- Will your core vendors agree to free or reduced shipping on orders of a certain dollar amount, or more?
- Will calling and attempting to 'cancel service' (whether you intend to or not) yield short-term deferrals or discounts?
- What is a vendor willing to offer to obtain more business from you, and take it away from another vendor (who may be less flexible)?
- Are group rates available, if employees want to add themselves to the service? (i.e. – cell phone providers)
- Are discounts available if something is purchased in bulk?
- Is there a price point close to what has been bid, that you may dictate for the vendor to accept? (i.e. – they quoted $20.00, but would they take $18.00, to accommodate your budget)?
- Will your bank agree to more favorable terms if you consolidate financial vehicles with their organization?
- Will a new bank 'beat' your current one, if you elect to move there?
- If you do change banks, new checks will be required – would they mind footing the bill for those?
- Is there an incentive program for referrals?
- Is there a loyalty program in place?
- Is the service provider willing to lock you in to this year's rate for a longer term?
- Can setup fees be waived?
- Can penalties be waived?
- Can an immediate settlement amount be reached?
- Are 'upgrades' available?
- Are quantity price breaks available, at certain purchase points?

You would be astounded how often the answer to all of the above is 'yes', or something appropriately akin to it. The reality is that most people never ask. Many feel that it's rude, or that it's counter-intuitive.

I understand that sentiment, but the fact is that if the individual or entity being asked doesn't like what you're asking, they have in their arsenal (as shown in the initial example) the word 'No'. That word is theirs to exercise whenever they choose during a negotiation. Sometimes you might hear it. More often than not, you won't.

Credit Cards: The Double-Edged Sword Of The Business World

Credit cards are bad. At least, that's what many folks are led to believe by their friends and family.

Television, on the other hand, does everything in its power to persuade you that they're all but a way to Heaven itself (with Alec Baldwin, no less!)

It's a strange dichotomy.

Credit cards can, if used improperly, be bad.

Credit cards, when used as the credit card companies intend, are bad.

Credit cards, when used the way I'm about to propose, can be very, very good.

A person who pays off their credit card balance every month has a name in the industry. And you won't believe what it is (well, unless you already know – then just act surprised). These people are known in the industry as 'deadbeats'.

Seriously – I can't make this stuff up.

I want to take a moment to encourage you to do something your parents would scold us for, if taken out of context. Be a deadbeat. More specifically, find a credit card that offers an incentive. Most already do, and the possibilities are as endless as they are (sometimes) weird.

In my case, I have a credit card issued through *Amazon.com*. Fifteen or so years ago, I chose this card because I was a bookaholic. It was right up my alley. It offered me 'points' on purchases, in differing tiers, depending on the product or service purchased. At the end of the month, I received a bill. I paid the bill. Once the money was transferred, I received 'points' that I could use to shop with on *Amazon.com*, in lieu of using money. I was in biblio-heaven.

Today, I'm far choosier about the few books that I buy. I also try to shop local, so I don't buy on *Amazon.com* as often. What I now do, is purchase everything that I possibly can on this card. I live on this card. I pay as many bills as those individuals sending them will permit me to with it. At the end of the month I receive my statement. I pay it in full. I receive my points. Then, I convert them back into a 'statement credit', to be applied in the next cycle. Essentially, I'm making money by using the credit card to its full potential.

My credit card offers me a simple, free method of purchasing just about anything, just about anywhere. I can monitor it on-line in real-time (which I do, because I'm paranoid – and you should as well). All of this, and – at the end of the cycle – they're giving me money for using it.

A business owner that's trying to make every cent count might find that this is a strategy that works well for them. And it doesn't have to be statement credits. Rewards, as I mentioned earlier, come in all kinds of kinds. Many people I know do what I do, but (since they run a far larger business) they rack up free airline miles and trips, instead. And it's crazy how fast you can make those points matter.

So before you dismiss using a credit card, consider being a deadbeat. It might be the best thing you ever disobeyed your parents over.

Calvin Coolidge, Perseverance, And You

Here's a pair of things that you might not think about, but you really should: research, and follow up.

My best examples of these two facets come from real-life experiences.

Remember that day job that I keep prattling on about?

It's a place where follow up contacts yield new customers each and every year. Here's how we make it work. The information below may be tailored to work for you as well.

First, we pay attention - abject tons of it. We find out what it is that our customers do. We research their web sites from top to bottom. Then, we further research anything that we don't understand or comprehend so that we may put it all together in our own minds. Then we do comprehensive searches on other businesses who are in the same industry, often in other states, who are not our customers (yet).

It's at this point that we create what we call a 'lead sheet'. This is submitted to our salesperson, with as much data as we can possibly glean.

Sometimes we find these leads by accident, coincidence, or even through referrals. The 'how' doesn't matter, really. What does matter is that we find them, and then proceed to arm ourselves with every piece of knowledge that we possibly can before a single sales call is made.

Then – and only then – do we move forward with the dreaded cold call. It's probably one of the most dehumanizing things that I've ever had to do. Not only do I hate doing them, I'm also really, really bad at them. Our outside sales staff perseveres where I falter.

Upon first contact with the company, our sales team may not even choose to speak with the appropriate party. Instead, they ask all the questions that they can, without being intrusive, gaining as much insight as they may. But this is only the next step of the process. Often this first call yields a contact name, and – hopefully – it will even yield crucial information.

Sometimes, one of our clerical staff will make a second call to ask different questions, if we don't feel that we got everything that we needed.

Why?

Different voice, different call = perception of non-linearity (i.e. – they have no idea it's the same organization calling them to gain more information.)

We wait a day, or two, or three, and then make yet another call. It is *now* that we ask for the individual whose name we gleaned from the first (or second) call. Now we've had time to tie up all of our research. Now our salesperson sounds like they might be a plausible caller. They often get through the normal backstops that insulate the buyers from cold calls.

More often than not, it's a call that ends in voicemail. This is not a bad thing. We've prepared for this eventuality. In my personal experience, it's often *better* than reaching the person whom you're calling. We offer a short, succinct, message about how we can *specifically* assist their needs (because we know what they do, and we've done our homework). We cite our relevant and unique experience. Occasionally, we may even 'name drop'. This usually serves to put this individual on notice that we're *already* serving companies in their field – possibly even their competition.

Then we let the phone call do what it will, while we move on - changing tactics. We have a packet of succinct data prepared that we send to potential clients, with short and to the point cover letter that serves to top it all off. Each of these is tailored to the client in question, so as to maximize their potential effect.

The hard reality is that there are a number of other companies out there who do what we do. The difference lies in *how* we do what we do, and what services (both primary and secondary) that we offer in-house that most of our competition doesn't. We take the opportunity to showcase those key differences, in the hopes of garnering their attention.

We follow up with periodic 'courtesy calls', depending upon the read we get from the potential client. If nothing comes of it, we ask if we may continue to contact them, periodically. Sometimes, we do so for years without a thing happening.

Then, magic happens. They get busy. They lose a vendor. They drop a vendor. Or – our favorite - the day comes when they have what we call a 'dead woodchuck*' project. It's on their desk, they haven't sourced it, it's a pain in their ass, and they want it gone. We happen to call, they look at it, perhaps having now forgotten the literature that we sent them, and they ask – specifically – if we can do anything with this damnable annoyance staring them in the face. This is where we pounce. We thrive on jobs like this, because we know that other shops shun them, and that it's a great way to showcase what we bring to the table.

*(Thanks to Scott Adams & *'Dilbert'* for that term - we use it all the time)

In every circumstance where this has happened, we go in (usually in person) and we wow them with our expertise. We send our company's Owner himself. A man who - though he hasn't been tested formally - I am certain is a genius. His experience is astounding, and his insight even more so. And when the potential client sees what an asset he potentially has in this person, and his company, they suddenly welcome us with open arms. It usually starts out slow, once the first project has been completed and delivered – on time and on budget, of course; a trickle of work. In some cases that trickle has led to six-figure per annum accounts. All of this happened because we did our homework, and we persevered.

Another method I have seen employed (which I don't use, personally) is the periodic letter.

I once had an insurance agency who was courting our business. What set them apart was that I would receive a short letter with a small piece of interesting or relevant information/facts/advice about once a month. This did two things: it disallowed my forgetting who they were, and showed me they really did want my business. They were crafting letters tailored to me, and even spending money on stamps: That impressed me.

The result?

They made our normally closed short list for quoting insurance. They didn't win the bid, but – unlike most – they at least had the opportunity.

I leave you now with one of my all-time favorite quotations from one of our lesser-known Presidents, Mr. Calvin Coolidge:

"Nothing in the world can take the place of Persistence. Talent will not; nothing is more common than unsuccessful men with talent. Genius will not; unrewarded genius is almost a proverb. Education will not; the world is full of educated derelicts. Persistence and determination alone are omnipotent. The slogan 'Press On' has solved – and always will – solve the problems of the human race."

Mr. Coolidge: I never knew you, but I respect and admire the heck out of you, sir. I wish that I had had the pleasure. My admiration for you will never diminish.

Reviewing Employee Performance Is More Than Checking Boxes: It's About Creating A Fundamentally Sound & Comprehensible Structure

How many of you have ever received a performance review?

Now bearing that question in mind, how many of you feel that you actually benefited from it in a non-monetary way?

Of those who did, how many feel that the company benefited from it also?

I'm betting that not many hands are raised just now (which is good, because I never once told you to raise them in the first place weirdoes).

When it comes to performance reviews, there really is no 'benchmark' or 'gold standard' to which we can attribute a set of solid, procedural, rules (at least, not one that I've yet found). As a result, most companies feel the inherent need to do them, yet few ever really comprehend why they're actually important - to both parties.

Allow me to, once more, tap my finite personal experiences to tell you a story. It's a very long one, but it also has a great many important points to offer up as to what not to do. See if you can pick up on them as the narrative flows:

When I was seventeen, I had graduated from high school, and had applied for a job at a national insurance carrier's claims office. I was invited back for a second interview, and was then required to complete several in-depth, aptitude and psychological tests. As the weeks wore on, I received word that I had not been selected for any of the open Medicare Claims Processing positions that I had applied for.

Two days later, I was notified by Human Resources that I had been bumped out of that queue of candidates intentionally, to be considered for a top-echelon, as-yet unadvertised, Major Medical Claims Processing job instead. I had no idea what this meant, but learned quickly that I had been selected to process the most labor-intensive and complex of all the policies that the company offered. Apparently, my test results were to their liking. To this day, I have never been privy to them.

With the promise of a 25% higher entry-level pay grade than the position that I had applied for, I of course took the job. Also, I needed a job, so I wasn't too fussy. Before I processed a single claim, I was put through the rigors of a six week, intensive, training experience that - truth be told - was no walk in the park.

Upon successful completion, I was put in the trenches. I very quickly went on to become the top producer in claims processing volume on the entire floor (which consisted of some two-hundred and thirty individuals in total). Not only was I the top producer, I was the top producer even against those who were processing the less complex policies (my numbers, when they needed help on *those policies*, actually broke daily processing records). On top of this, I *always* took the extra time to set up the back-end, tracking pages for each customer's account I accessed that did not yet have them done. This was viewed as insanity by my co-workers, as it sapped time from my bottom line numbers. It made sense to me, because it was just good etiquette to do so for the sake of 'ease of use' for the next Claims Processor to access the account. Couple that with the fact that we had been asked to specifically do so in training, and I had no intention of not complying with this reasonable request.

For a year, I continued - week after week, month after month - hitting my quality quotients, and being the top producer on the floor by a wide margin. Before the year was over, I was the only non-supervisor who was permitted to process - without any formal oversight - a claim valued at up to $25,000. This was $15,000 more than any other non-supervisor on the floor. So, when the time came for my first performance review, I wasn't sure what to expect. It was my first time experiencing one in such a corporate environment. One thing I knew for certain: I expected to be rewarded.

Here is where my first point of advice comes in. As an employer, make certain that your expectations of performance are outlined up front, at the time of hire. Identify what criteria will be used to evaluate the employee, what will and won't count against their ability to receive a raise, etc. This takes some time and thought, but it also gives your employees some known benchmarks to shoot for, with the goal being to please you, and – in the process of doing so - better themselves monetarily and experientially.

Here's how my first performance review went down: I was told that all employees in Major Medical Claims were entitled to a maximum of a 3% raise that year. This was the first time that I had heard this, but shame on me for not having asked before then (my early working life was full of valuable learning experiences like this). I was told everything about my performance that I already knew. I didn't get to speak. My supervisor went over my production numbers, quality percentages, and attendance record with rote efficiency. Then, she congratulated me, and told me that I was to receive a 2% (out of a potential 3%, recall) raise.

Short of my wife saying, "I do", this was the most shocking thing that I have ever heard in my life. To say I was taken aback is a grave injustice to the gravity I felt the situation imposed upon me. I was literally floored by what had just left this woman's lips.

So I did what every know-it-all seventeen year-old would do: I promptly asked why, and let my indignation show. Her response floored me further. Part of the raise criteria, I was informed, was based upon how well an employee was socially adapted to working with other employees.

I asked how that worked, as we each had individual cubicles, and were encouraged to listen to music while we worked.

Her response was that while I did superior work, it was her impression that I didn't go out of my way to commiserate with my fellow employees during break times. In fact, I often was seen not taking them at all. On random, potluck, days, I chose not to participate. This was seen as an alienating of comrades in the workplace and, therefore, anti-social behavior.

To be fair - it was just that.

Here's the problem: I was seventeen, fresh out of high school, not a lunch eater, and a broke kid who still lived in a home where ends barely met. I had three changes of dress clothes to my name. My co-workers were predominantly in their late twenties to late thirties, with families, and a great many of them were females who were - or whose husbands were - well-off. I was made fun of by some of the most self-professed religious members in my group about my clothing, and really had no social desire to connect with such shallow and - to my way of thinking - boring and pretentious creatures. They often went out drinking socially. At seventeen, I was the lone individual in my group who could not join them. So - no, damn it - I did not socialize. Point well noted.

That, my friends, is how I found myself in transition. The 2% was a done deal, and I was told that I could take it up with the VP if I wished further action to be taken.

Clueless teen that I was, I did just that.

That meeting was worse, because I was - once more - lauded for my performance, and told that the original decision was up to the supervisor. No overruling would be forthcoming.

Then, I did something that decidedly showed my tender age. I asked the VP, "So, then, what's my motivation?"

The answer from the VP was, honest to God, "I don't know."

That tore it. I applied for the next open position in Claims Customer Service - a semi-lateral, step down. The move was granted, and I underwent a further four weeks of intensive training. I was told that I was the only employee - at that time - who had ever made this odd move. Most, in fact, had made the opposite move: beginning in Claims Customer Service, and then transferring to Major Medical Claims Adjudication.

I was also the only employee on the Claims Customer Service floor who had the claims system accessible to me. The reason was that I had been 'invited' to work all the overtime that I wished, upstairs in claims, when my normal workday in Claims Customer Service was over. This was in an effort to continue to address the more than three-month backlog of claims that remained unprocessed, due to acquisitions the company had made in te past two years.

During live call training I found, on several occasions, situations where I had to correct the individual doing the training.* I actually got excited, once I was put on the phones.

Why?

I felt like I could make a significant difference to people, here. Here, someone on the other end of the line would appreciate my help. Granted, many were cranky (who isn't usually cranky with customer service?) but I considered their situations rom their side of things. More often than not, we ended the call amicably.

*(At one point, I had to fight with the 'trainer' that a claim wasn't about drugs being denied - it was about durable medical equipment - and that that code wasn't an arcane drug reference but was, in fact, an HCPCS code. I received a very blank stare for my efforts.)

In Claims Customer Service, when a claim had been processed incorrectly, we had been instructed to route it through Major Medical Claims anew, with an addendum citing what we wished for them to reconsideration. My callers didn't have to wait, though. Often, I could switch over into the claims system, fix the issue, and have it done before we disconnected. I made a lot of cranky people very, very happy. I actually liked coming to work. Life was good.

While many of my callers were thrilled, my supervisor was the opposite. I was written up for the first time in my life, a week later, for having done the above. It was cited by him as a breach of protocol.

The seventeen year-old know-it-all argued that it was, in fact, no such thing - I had access to claims for a reason, and why drag these poor soul's misery out longer, when I could fix the problem, right then and there?

This only served to single me out further. I was written up a second time about month later. The reason this time was that I was 'coming to work late'.

What I was, in fact, doing was signing on to my phone later than 8:00 am. Their expectation was that I would punch in on floor one, come upstairs, open all of my software, log in to my terminal, check my mail, and get my day ready to rock, and then be signed on to my phone and taking calls at precisely 8:00 am.

I mentioned that I only got paid from 8:00 on, regardless of when I signed on to my phone. As such, all the time spent from when I punched in, until I signed on to my phone (the super-majority of which was spent doing work things) would, then, become free to the company. I didn't understand how this was fair to me.

Two weeks later, I quit. It was the only job I ever just walked away from. My Mother and friends thought that I was nuts for walking away from a job that paid so well. Perhaps I was. I'd just like to think that I was the right kind of nuts. In hindsight, it was one of the most astute decisions that I've ever made.

All right, story's over. Now: Remember those points I asked you to look for? Here's my tally of them:

- The company lost its record-setting, top claims producer
- The company spent a cumulative total of ten weeks training me, with pay
- The company lost a high-dollar claims releaser, who could ease the burden upon the supervisors by processing these without bothering them
- The company lost a person who gave up break time to simply continue working
- The company lost an individual who wasted ZERO time on potluck chatter, eating, and general participation
- The company lost a potential candidate for a supervisory role
- The company lost a Customer Service Agent who wielded more ability to help than anyone else, save one of the four supervisors in

that department
- The company lost the recouping of valuable time and resources by keeping the claims reconsideration lanes a little clearer
- The company lost a claims adjudicator who could process all of the claim types on offer, including the most difficult (which was rare)

To me, this is an outrageous injustice to the company. They spent so much money and time on me, and then drove me out via inaction, ineptitude, and inflexibility. Maybe I'm in a minority for thinking this. The reason for this long, self-aggrandizing, story is this: performance reviews are ridiculously important.

As an employer it is incumbent upon you to create an environment of checks and balances that make sense to all parties involved. Create clear and concise criteria for your employees to be judged upon, and then follow through and do so. If an employee's actions are not as desired, correct them, and make note of it. One thing that I can't stress enough is that a performance review is like a crime scene. In the end, it will require good evidence to make your case. Likewise, your employees can be a phenomenal resource for learning about shortcomings or areas for improvement in your business. I treat my performance reviews like a courtroom battle. I come in prepared to explain to my employer why I feel I deserve a raise, what I have done to deserve it (that he may or may not be aware of), and so on. And he, being an employer who understands the value of this input, not only listens, but on occasion of agreement, acts upon my suggestions or information. Can you say the same for yourself as an employer?

If you want your employees to work as you wish, then give them rock-solid goals, benchmarks, and job descriptions. Then, come review time, hear their side. Then be prepared to voice your own. Explain what helped or hindered their raise - or level of raise - so that they have a clear idea of what they should be working on for future reviews.

Another fallacy is that a performance review should be given annually. Sometimes, this isn't enough. I personally find that quarterly reviews are a much more intelligent method to employ, as they allow for faster action upon potential problem areas, more knowledge can be gleaned about the parts of your business that go 'unseen' by you, and so on. I would recommend keeping the raise aspect annual, but by doing quarterly sit-downs with employees, you can continue to offer suggestions on how they might attain the greatest return by pleasing you, and meeting your needs.

In conclusion, take the time to formulate and execute a plan for reviews. Share it with employees. Be prepared to back up your findings during the review process. Be open minded with their suggestions. If you can't act upon them, you don't always have to explain why, but doing so can often have no negative impact on the situation. Consider the investment of time and capital that you have placed in an individual when considering evaluations. The last thing you want to do is alienate, frustrate, or upset them to the degree that they seek employment elsewhere. At that point, the new employer wins, because all of those resources that you allocated become theirs for nothing, in the form of the experience taken with the individual upon departure.

70

If you're not doing performance reviews with these thoughts in mind, then I strongly encourage you to take a serious look at your business model. Make a plan to succeed - for you, for the business, and for the business' employees by making the employees that you already have accountable, rewarded, feeling valued, validated, heard, and happy.

The 'Save The Employee' Mentality

Many businesses grow beyond the cottage stage. There comes a point in the life-cycle of a business when a decision needs to be made: to hire, or not to hire.

If your business already has employees, or if you ever consider your business as a candidate that will require them, then listen up. Employees cost a lot more than you may think, and are also more valuable than you imagine. This phenomena goes far beyond the basics of wages or salaries, Medicare & Social Security taxes, benefits, state & federal unemployment taxes, workman's compensation insurance, and business insurance. For every employee that you welcome to the team, there are often additional expenses that go unnoticed. To recap from earlier sections:

- Advertising for the position
- Interviewing for the position
- Paying additional unemployment insurance, based on date of hire and whether or not this individual is replacing someone else
- Training
- Lack of productivity during the learning period (often on the part of the trainer, and the trainee)
- Additional resources to do the job correctly

With all of this in mind, it is incumbent upon you to do everything within your power, and within reason, to retain current employees. No matter how out of control a situation may seem, the employee still has a value. The question you have to ask yourself is, 'Is this individual costing me more than they're worth?'

This is assuming the worst - that the employee is somehow not meeting your expectations. Let's focus on this facet for a moment. With a sensible checks and balances system in place, you can often reign in the employee by enacting verbal warnings, written warnings, suspensions, lack of financial reward, other penalization, or demotion. Many times, these deterrents will be enough to turn an employee around, and assist them in continuing to be profitable. If none of this works, and you've reached a point of irreconcilable differences then - and only then - can you truly say that you've done everything that you may, and watch as the employee moves on - voluntarily or otherwise.

71

A far worse scenario is when a profitable, or even worse outstanding, employee notifies you that he or she is leaving the fold for greener pastures. A great many employers will allow this to signal an official end to their mutually beneficial relationship. A truly good employer will parse out the situation to its most finite components.

Believe it or not, leaving can be as much, or even more, of a hassle for the employee as it is for you. And this is where the 'Save the Employee' mentality enters the picture.

Why are they leaving?

Is it something that you are financially or otherwise prepared to negate?

Is that option even on the table for the exiting employee?

Once this assessment has been made, you stand a very good chance of retaining the employee. If failure to do so is the outcome, you now have that much more insight into the employee's way of thinking. This may hold future value.

Consider all of these things before firing off the cuff or, allowing an employee to simply turn in their two-week's notice, unfettered. It's in your best interest to try and salvage your relationship. It may, ultimately, be in theirs as well.

Promotion From Within: What Not To Do

Envision this scenario: you work in a company of ten individuals, all doing the same job. You're the employee with the most seniority. A new position comes open that affords upward mobility to the 'next level' in the company. You are passed over for it. Another employee, who arrived three years after you, is chosen to fill it.

You're pissed, right?

Well, if you're not, then you're not like most people. Most people have a preconceived notion of how promotion within a business works. And, sadly, it usually centers around two things:

- Having a degree
- Having seniority

You might hate me for saying this, but here we go: that's a stupid way to do things.

Why is it stupid?

I want you to change mental gears for a moment. Now imagine that you're the owner of that company that just promoted someone. Do you pick an individual whose sole qualification is a piece of paper, or longevity? Sadly, most businesses do. But that's a long-practiced idiocy that's now beginning to see some serious change (though not soon enough, if you ask me).

The fact of the matter is that you began your business to (in essence) enjoy life more, and tap everything that you've got to give the world at large. So why in the world would you entrust the senior individual, solely because of said seniority, without considering other facets?

It's lunacy.

The senior-most person might very well be the best person for the job – don't get me wrong, here. Often, that individual knows the business better than others who came along later.

A college graduate is perceived to have a higher level of education, and perseverance than the average Joe Lunchpail. Therefore, they must be smarter, and more capable. That's the fallacy. That's the persistent and prevalent stereotype.

I'm going to give you some real-world examples for you to consider. I'm going to use the personal experiences of both myself, and of my amazing wife.

My wife once worked for an international corporation. She liked it there. When she hired in, however, there was no room for upward mobility in the company for her. She didn't have a degree, and that was the key to that mobility. In the end, the company lost a stellar employee, who now has a job where the employer recognized sheer talent, and effectively said, "Perhaps the degree isn't the only thing we should consider." If I haven't mentioned it before, she is in contact with the White House, Senators, Congressmen, celebrities, and other worldwide movers and shakers. She has been certified as an expert in everything *Microsoft* can throw at an individual working in an office. She can design web pages. She's a certified Paralegal, she types 90+ words per minute. She's well-versed in more software than most folks know exist. She runs her own not-for-profit organization. She handles the entire web arm of our business. She can arrange anything, world-wide, with a simple demand to do so. She is the personal assistant to one of the most powerful, and notable, men in our state, who also has a national, and international, presence as well.

There are a million other things that my wife can do, any five of which most folks will never be able to say in a lifetime that they, too, can. The

GUERRILLA BUSINESS ♦ HEATH D. ALBERTS

reason I'm telling you this, is to prove a point: was that degree really that important, in the end?

Sadly, the corporation lost her to greener pastures.

Happily, someone who 'gets it' snatched her up.

I, too, was a multiple 'victim' of this seniority/degree phenomena. Thankfully, I found my place in life, and work for a fellow who seeks only to surround himself with those who can perform numerous tasks well, and efficiently.

73

I've departed corporations who have played the seniority/degree game. I have a great many skills, which – on paper – seem like someone is just making things up as they go.

I've witnessed, powerless, as individuals that I know personally have been hired into positions that I could never apply for, even though I know that I'm far better qualified, skilled, and motivated*.

*(I don't begrudge them anything - I'm happy for them!)

I could go into great detail, but I think the point is made. Greatness does not come from obtaining a piece of paper, or being somewhere the longest. Greatness is forged in desire, acumen, intellect, skill, and drive. Greatness is a state of mind, and a constant striving to better oneself.

If you're hiring – or promoting – using only seniority or degrees as criteria, then you're taking a large risk. It's a risk that vacillates between becoming a great company or in remaining a mediocre one.

The Exit Interview: The Black Sheep Of The Business World

Losing an employee, valuable or not, can be like a messy break up. It can be socially awkward. It can uncomfortable for not only the parties involved, but the secondary parties (i.e. - the co-workers) as well. It is something that can go completely unnoticed in a mega-corporation, or rock a small business to its very foundation. For the most part, it's a generally unpleasant experience for all involved.

If you have done all that you may, and the decision is still set for imminent departure, then take one last opportunity to learn something from this individual before you part ways. Enter, the exit interview*.

*(Clever phrasing - achieved!)

Exit Interviews come in all shapes and sizes. Even with all of the myriad jobs that I've held over the years, I - personally - have never been given one. Which, to some degree, is a shame. I feel like I had a lot to offer in the way of advice. I might not have, but it makes me feel more important to pretend, nonetheless.

Ah, narcissism.

>AHEM<

Preparation for the exit interview can be nothing more than finding a quiet area to have a candid chat in. Conversely, it could be the formulation and creation of a series of pointed questions to tease out information that, under normal circumstances (or without copious amounts of alcohol having first been imbibed), employees would never be so forthcoming with.

Above all else, the employee must feel comfortable. They must know that you want and need them to be brutally honest. What comes from this experience might hurt your feelings; might confuse or confound you. Keep that all in check. The employee will be less hindered, if you seem levelheaded; interested in what he or she has to say.

And for goodness sake, listen to them!

This is a perfect opportunity for you to find out about things in the workplace that others may never mention: a tyrannical manager; an inept co-worker; an unsafe condition; fear of vampires in the janitor's closet. Tough though it may be to hear, don't exclude yourself from the line of fire, either. You may come to find, in a rare moment of free candor, that the problem is - in fact - staring you in the face every time a mirror is in front of you. Unless you're a vampire, in which case you're probably also the problem, especially if you've been hanging out in the janitor's closet.

Whatever the outcome, plan to act upon the specifics that you feel you have control over. If something is mentioned as lacking, consider adding it. If something is broken in the social hierarchy of the business, take this opportunity to fix or address it before you lose someone else due to its continued existence. If ineptitude is perceived to exist, keep a closer eye on the culprit. If vampires really *are* in the janitor's closet, buy some garlic and contact a reputable stake company. Failure to act upon the information supplied, means failing to rectify situations that may cause further exodus down the road. And no one - not even your employees - wants that.

Part 2: Think Outside The Box - Way Outside, Even

Let's make a Meme-ory

Ah, memes.

Wait, what?

You don't know what a meme is?

Well, let's fix that first, then. According to *WikiPedia*:

"An Internet Meme is an idea that is propagated through the World Wide Web. The idea may take the form of a hyperlink, video, picture, website, hashtag, or just a word or phrase, such as intentionally misspelling the word "more" as "moar" or "the" as "teh". The meme may spread from person to person via social networks, blogs, direct email, news sources, or other web-based services.

An Internet meme may stay the same or may evolve over time, by chance or through commentary, imitations, parody, or by incorporating news accounts about itself. Internet memes can evolve and spread extremely rapidly, sometimes reaching world-ide popularity within a few days. Internet memes usually are formed from some social interaction (such as rage comic or reaction faces), pop culture reference (such as Pardon the Interruption's Tony Kornheiser in WHY.jpg, Xzibit in "Yo Dawg," or situations people often find themselves in (such as "That feel when," Socially Awkward Penguin, and Futurama Fry / Not Sure If X). Sometimes these categories cross over, as with Futurama Fry, and costanza.jpg, a popular reaction face of George Costanza from Seinfeld. Many memes also come from video games (such as the "arrow to the knee" from The Elder Scrolls V: Skyrim or "Do a barrel roll" from Starfox 64) or the scene from "Downfall". For researchers it's hard to track down the birthplace of memes because of their viral nature, as well as the high chance that the meme will spread to major websites nearly instantly.

Their rapid growth and impact has caught the attention of both researchers and industry.[3] Academically, researchers model how they evolve and predict which memes will survive and spread throughout the Web. Commercially, they are used in viral marketing where they are an inexpensive form of mass advertising."

So what does this mean to you?

Well, perhaps nothing.

Or perhaps it means that you're now obtaining a basic understanding of your next big - and free! - marketing idea.

For you see, memes gain momentum dependent upon the strength of the concept put forth. For our purposes, let's focus for a moment on one of the more prevalent meme phenomena - that of the photograph.

By itself, a photograph can be fairly mundane. However, if one were to meme-ifiy it by adding quasi-relevant, humorous text, it becomes a whole new ball game. I'm willing to bet that somewhere you have an insane photograph in storage that is just begging for a caption to bring it to life. I know personally that I have an amazing photo of my Great Aunt that she accidentally took of herself at an up-the-nose-angle while trying to figure out how to use the disposable cameras we offered up at our wedding. If I didn't love and respect her, I would be all over meme-ing the living crap out of it.

So, how about you?

Am I generating any ideas yet?

When it comes to memes, social media is your most powerful ally. By creating - and imparting - a new meme via social media channels, you're tapping into a cluster of friends, family, and acquaintances who have the power to spread your meme virally across myriad layers of friends-of-friends-of-friends, etc. *This* is where you ultimately want to end up.

So find that money shot (no, not that kind, perv-o) photo. Using any software that you might have - from *MS Paint*, to higher-end products - simply add a caption that's funny. If you're not funny, I'd be willing to bet that you know someone who is. Another option would be to have a caption contest in your store, or anywhere the public has an opportunity to interact with you.

The important part is to – somehow - tie the meme back to yourself/your business. This can be done by adding your URL, *FaceBook* page link, or other link (and your logo as well) in an unobtrusive area of the meme photo. The object is not only to entertain, but to get folks to visit the launch pad of this new, humorous creation in an attempt to gain a new audience, and, hopefully, new business.

And who's to say that you have to stop at just one?

In fact, when it comes to memes, building an audience that looks forward to regular output is a much stronger - and lasting - option. If possible, prepare a number of them, all at one time, and release them slowly. I would recommend seeing how long it takes to generate new hits and likes, and gauge it from there. It may be days, or weeks. Whatever you do, don't wait too long. This will have those once-interested individuals scattering for greener pastures. Especially if your target audience is like me, with no attention span and... oh, look! A bird!

So find that photo, get creative, and be funny. I promise that you - and those who enjoy it - won't regret it.

The Envelope, Please!

I attended a Christmas party a while back, held at a local upscale restaurant. The food, company, and setting were all quite nice. As the final round of dishware was being cleared, a waitress came around to all of the couples and individuals. From a basket on her arm, she handed each a sealed, red envelope. Aside from being festively printed, and intriguing, here is what the envelope read:

"Come back to <Restaurant> any time between <dates> and bring this envelope - unopened - to receive one of six secret prizes! Envelope needs to be opened in front of your server to be valid."

It then went on to list the prizes:

- A $100 Gift Certificate
- A $50 Gift Certificate
- A Free Entree Up To $22
- $15 Off Of Your Check
- A Free Appetizer
- $5 Off Of Your Check

Frankly?
The food itself was enough to bring me back.
But with this addition?
This was a stroke of pure genius. Consider how many folks will be swayed off of the fence, in the hopes of hitting the big one. You're guaranteed something, as well. I like that idea.

While it may not sway everyone, it was such a unique and interesting idea that I felt that I couldn't avoid sharing it. It has all the hallmarks of a true guerrilla endeavor:

- It offers incentive
- It offers intrigue
- It's not hokey, like some 'giveaways' or 'contests'
- It's straightforward
- It had great presentation

The return on investment could be phenomenal, if it succeeds as I believe it will. Congratulations to this establishment. It proves that guerrilla marketing is for every business, no matter the clientele, and can be done - and done well - when the proper facets are collectively applied.

Go Ninja On Your Local Bookstore!

As a self-published author, I used to go to used bookstores. There, I would seek out books that were in the same genre/vein as the one which I had written. For just this occasion, I had developed a two-sided bookmark, outlining everything about my book, as well as a short biography of myself, and placed them in all of the books that I felt were highly likely to be purchased by my target market.

I would caution that this is probably best done in used bookstores, rather than new ones, but either will do. What's extremely compelling about this tactic is that it can be tied to nearly any topic available in your average bookstore, and can also be accomplished with only a small cost being incurred.

And it doesn't have to be a bookmark, though the practicality of the item does lend itself to not being thrown away out of hand. It can be a sticker (left on the sticker's backing, of course - otherwise you're damaging property, and I won't be held liable for that sort of thing), a business card, or a photo. It's all dependent upon the product, and the information that you wish to impart to your potential clientele.

Another variant on this notion would be to contact the store owner, and find out if they would be willing to either allow you to dispense bookmarks in their store, or split the costs of having some made, with bilateral advertising on them. This brings more of a sense of 'propriety' to the table, but sort of takes all of the James Bond, cloak and dagger fun out of seeding the books.

Reward: Missing Unicorn

My wife and I were in downtown Dubuque, Iowa a few months back for a wedding. As we explored the downtown area, we saw a number of 'lost pet' signs that had been posted on power and phone poles, as well as in the bus stop vestibules. We stopped to abide a red light. It was then that I took more notice of the poster, and was floored by what I saw.

The poster was a marketing tool. The headline read, "*Lost Unicorn*" and did, in point of fact, have a headshot of a unicorn, front and center. Below this was 'contact' information for the store responsible, as well as sales information.

Not only did this guerrilla sign get our attention, but we actually took the time to get out of our car and see what it was all about. Heck, we even took a picture. *This* is guerrilla marketing in full effect, and I cannot tell you how impressed I was with this simple, yet effective, tactic.

Plus, they might even have gotten a unicorn out of the deal.

Who knows?

The Poor Man's Billboard

Ever wish you had the capital to purchase billboard space?

Yeah – me too.

But wait - maybe, you do!

Here's how:

Find someone with a decent fence, who also happens to live next door to a fast food restaurant, shopping center, box store, or other establishment that receives a ton of unique eyeballs on a daily basis. Have a banner made at a local vinyl place (or something akin), and contact the owner of said fence. Offer them a flat rate per month, a one-time rate, or a percentage of income, to allow you to post the sign on the establishment-side of the fence. It might cost a couple hundred dollars – but it's exponentially less than purchasing a billboard. The longer it stays in place, the better your return on investment becomes.

Halloween May Be Your Turn To Trick - And Treat Yourself

When Halloween approaches, why not make the holiday tax-deductible?

Try this idea on for size: find a promotional item – let's say a mini-*Frisbee* – and give them out either in place of, or with, candy. Make sure your logo and slogan are front and center. Then, the adults in the children's lives will, at the very least, see it once. They'll probably see it again and again – in the garage, when they clean their kid's room, when they play with their children with it, etc. It's a small price to pay for multiple exposures, and a unique way to market to a wide variety of individuals.

Become A Prevalent Voice In Your Niche

This one is a little more daring, but viable, nonetheless. *Amazon.com* (and, more recently, other outlets) offers self-publishing services via their *CreateSpace* and *Kindle Direct Publishing* arms. You can actually submit a digital manuscript to them, use their cover designer, and print a book – all for free.

Why bother?

Well, if you have something authoritative to offer, the book doesn't have to be long (24 pages is their minimum) – just relevant.

Imagine being the individual who literally 'wrote the book' on something?

This obviously isn't for everyone – but oh, what a marketing tool! Plus, if it's good enough, you'll even make a few extra bucks when the book sells. You can also set it up for e-readers, and even sell copies wherever your products are sold, or in stores that offer local goods for sale.

Jones Soda: A Reciprocal Relationship Waiting To Happen

Did you know that the *Jones Soda Company* allows submissions of the public's photos for consideration of being placed upon their bottles' labels?

Also, they allow you to submit photos and purchase your own 'customized' bottles, even if they don't choose your photo for a production run. It's an interesting way to market yourself. You can sell said bottles at fairs and festivals in your booth, or find a current *Jones* vendor who might be willing to put your bottles in place of others they would otherwise buy for their own stock. I'm sure that there tons of clever things that you could do, depending on your product!

Turn Something Of Questionable Taste Into Something Brilliant

This idea may be a little out of season (depending upon when you're reading this), but to be fair I can't be held responsible for when you decide to read this, can I?

I'm actually just thankful that my brain keeps cranking these ideas out, or this book would be pretty mundane, boring, and populated by tumbleweeds.

That, and Weird Uncle Pete looking for...

You know what?

Never mind.

Getting back to the idea: everyone's seen those mostly stupid looking (yeah, you heard me – cope with my disgust) cardboard window 'thingies' to keep the sun out of your car.

How about finding a blank one (or blanking one out, and doing society a favor).

I mean, do we really needs an 80's-esque collage of flamingos and... what?

All right, all right.

My wife says, "Get to the point, and stop ranting!"

So, what if you 'modified' one to be a billboard for your business?

Every time you used it, someone would see it, and your car stays cool (figuratively and literally, because now the flamingos are, mercifully for all involved, gone).

You might even consider giving some to your relatives and friends to gain even more exposure.

What have you got to lose?

(Except those stupid fla... ouch! She pinched me! I can't believe she pinched me! And now she's dragging me... hey... *hey*, I....!

Facebook & Blogs: 24-Hour, 365.25-Day Per-annum, Venues

Many of us have experienced it. We craft what we feel to be a brilliant post in a blog, *Facebook* group, or *Facebook* page, only to see it languish without a single response like a loquacious person on a raft in the middle of the ocean. Conversely, we can post the most inane, random things, and it somehow turns into a monstrous thread that ends in talk about pudding recipes and Weird Uncle Pete's recent arrest.

Have any of you ever considered why this is?

And if you have, have you ever considered the old adage, '*Timing is everything?*'

If not, then consider this: Individuals who are on the web, or *Facebook*, are on when it's convenient for them to be on. Just because you're on at 3 am while watching Monkey Polo on *ESPN* Nine and eating ice cream from the container, doesn't mean that the rest of the world is. Likewise, your core demographic may not be on Sunday mornings, while your heathen-self is at home browsing Weird Uncle Pete's latest web shenanigans.

Still, there are ways to combat this. First – and foremost – take a look back at your better-response-producing threads.

At what time did they occur?

What day was it?

Was it a holiday?

Parsing out the data in such a manner should begin to reveal some semblance of a pattern.

Further, you can even do the unthinkable: ask for your user's opinions. Just ask them when they're on most, and begin compiling the data. If the folks who answer that they're on in a certain time frame are mostly looky-loo's, then change gears. You want to find out when the individuals you most wish to reach are around. This will give you the best chances of their reading, commenting, re-posting, or inviting their friends into the fold. This, in turn, will lead to growth and an expanded audience that you actually want to hear you.

Facebook also offers a number of quantification metrics on pages that prove extremely helpful in this endeavor as well – so use them!

So do yourself a favor - be careful when you post!

Save the 'best stuff' for the peak times, and leave the random musings about lint that looks like celebrities for those Sunday mornings when the tumbleweeds and crickets are more prolific.

Go Ninja On Public PC's

This idea is a bit in the 'dark-grey area' of things – so don't do something stupid. In fact, pretend that I'm there, standing over your shoulder, dressed like a nun and wielding a stout-looking ruler.

Would I whack you, or turn a blind eye for what you're about to do?

With that in mind, the idea:

82

Computers are everywhere: stores, libraries, in a friend's home during a party, and on and on. Most of them are locked up tighter than Fort Knox - but not all of them. If you find one that's manipulate-able, open the browser and go to your web site.

Then, walk away.

If you're even luckier, and it's wide open, make your site the home page. And – again – walk away.

Imagine your web site, seen by all of the shoppers or passers-by (until someone changes it – but hopefully they're lazy). It's a cheap way to get eyeballs on your business, without really hurting anything, or anyone. And the *ASPCA* won't even bug you, because no animals were harmed.

Go Ahead - Fill Someone Else's Void

I'll just assume that you've just made a dirty joke in your mind.

If you didn't then we probably wouldn't get along too well in the real world.

>AHEM<

Hotels, truck stops, libraries, public buildings, restaurants, and museums all have something in common: pamphlet racks. And those racks are seldom completely full.

So why not 'help out' by filling a space?

Create some inexpensive (but also of the best quality that you can afford) pamphlets on your computer using *MS Word*, *MS Publisher*, *Serif Page*, *MS Excel*, a similar piece of software, or a professional service, and place them in these locations, periodically. If you plan to do this long-term, make sure to note, whenever possible, statistical data (how many remain, how long it's been since your last visit, etc.) so as to keep your time spent replenishing to a minimum.

Your Home Windows: Boring As Heck, Or Exciting Advertising Medium?

Do you live on a busy street?

If not, that's all right - just not as desirable for this idea.

Make your front window(s) a nighttime showpiece!*

*(For this idea, you might need help from a local printer or artist).

Create a window-sized, semi-opaque (or semi-transparent, for all you optimists out there), screen that can be backlit at night to create a virtual 'lighted sign'. It can be changed, moved, colored differently (light bulbs do, in fact, come in colors - you need to get out more if you didn't know that), and on and on!

So long as your city, town, or local government doesn't prohibit it (make sure that you check first!) you've now set yourself up to garner the attention of hundreds, or thousands, of evening driver's bored eyeballs.

Inverse Protests & You

Protesters. You know, those individuals with an agenda and signs. Yeah: those folks.

What would happen if you held a 'Reverse Protest' outside of your place of business?

The idea goes something like this:

You get some friends and family, and, heck, even Weird Uncle Pete can hold a sign! You make up some signs stating specifics of the Reverse Protest like, "*Customer Service Here Is Too Good!*", "*This Place Offers Service That Is Too Gracious And Focused On Your Needs!*"

On the surface, it sounds insane. But – think about it - you *will* get noticed. Heck, you might even get local media coverage for the stunt (and a phone call ahead of time won't hurt that, either).

Share Your Expertise, And Reap The Free Benefits

Are you an expert on the mating habits of the fruit fly?

Do you know how to make fire with only corn chips and a hole punch?

Show off *your* specific expertise – whatever it may be – by participating in forums or groups related specifically to themes involving your products or services. Then, drive traffic back to your website through your forum or group signature.

Presto!

Potential new customers, blog followers, or *Facebook* subscribers appear. Remember this, though: just because you have them at that moment, doesn't mean that they'll stay. Give them a good reason through insightful blogs, coupons, discounts, or anything entertaining that works within your business model to keep them around – and coming back.

Make Your Mail Scream, "*Pick Me! Pick Me!*"

Make your mail something unique. Often in my research, I see mentioned the trick of using a lot of one-cent stamps.

To that, I say, "Meh. Not good enough."

Sure, it might be interesting: but not interesting *enough*. Here's a different (read: better) approach:

When I was a kid, I used to send away to baseball players for their autographs. Before I did, though, I hand wrote a thoughtful letter thanking them for being awesome. Then I spent as many as four hours turning the plain, white, #10 envelope into a 360º work of full-color art.

And do you know what?

All but *ONE* came back, in all the years I did this (bite me, Walt Weiss of the *Oakland A's*). In fact, I obtained some signatures that other individuals, and even trade publications, had confided were real toughies (or even impossible) to get through the mail. Further, I got them *FAST*. It doesn't take a genius to figure out that in a sea of white, the painstaking work of art will get noticed first.

Back to the real world, where I'm all grown up now: when we began *Digital Ninjas Media, Inc.*, I had one thought in the first week that stuck with me. I was going to do something like this again. So I got on line, and looked for solid BLACK #10 envelopes.

And you know what?

I found them. They're a ridiculous .30 cents apiece – but I found them - and I bought them.

Want to really make your cold correspondence something potentially deify-able?

Find a local artist whose work is impressive, and ask to purchase the rights to a work. Take it to a printing house that can do custom envelopes and have it made into said-same.

Imagine your initial response, if you opened your mailbox, and found something visually stunning in amongst the day-to-day postal flotsam?

Turn Your Voice Mail Demons Into Viral Marketing Tools

Voice mail - there, I've said it.

Are you happy now?

I >*HATE*< voice mail. Hate it, hate it, hate it, hate it. Oh, and, also: I H-A-T-E I-T!

Sometimes, however, it's a necessary evil. Hey – it happens. I'm not here to judge. In fact, we here at *Digital Ninjas Media, Inc.* even have it, but only because we have to.

If you're stuck with it, as we are, then why not make the most of it?

Begin by leaving the canned message. Make sure that you advise what to press to leave a message, and then over-encourage that the caller do so.

Then leave a few seconds of dead air. Here, at this moment, is where the magic happens. An addendum to the canned message occurs:

"*Okay. Now that those folks in a hurry are gone…,*" and then something truly funny needs to ensue for this to work. *Nestlé*, for example, has had great success with this, by offering funny options in pig-Latin on their hotline, as well as some other goofy stuff.

How do I know?

It went viral, and I called it. It was a number that I would never have called.

The viral stuff?

Yeah, it worked on me.

Once the message is in place, take a moment to 'leak' to your friends that it's there. If it's good enough, they'll tell their friends, etc. and soon it goes viral and gets out of control. And suddenly, everyone has heard of you, or your business.

Nominate Yourself - I Won't Judge You (Double Meaning - Achieved!)

"And this year's >Insert Obscure Award Name Here< goes to - you!"

In this day and age, there are awards for almost anything and everything that you can think of. Well, okay – not *everything* – but you get my meaning.

So why not see if there's an award that's relevant or germane to what you're doing?

Perhaps it's local. Perhaps it's national. Or, if you're really lucky, it functions as both.

Take the time to find out who offers it, what it takes to be considered for it, and then do that!

Who knows?

You might even win. And how cool would *that* look on your marketing materials?

Even if no one knows what the '*Herb Scrumford-Tally Cup*' is, saying you won something gains you a new modicum of respect and prestige. It's just how we're wired as people, for the most part: we like award winners.

Connect With Categorical Royalty: A Case Study

I recently spent a solid weekend doing several 'guerrilla' things.

The end result?

I've connected with over 1,200 published authors on *Facebook* - including Tim Dorsey, Douglas Preston, George Pelecanos, Lincoln Child, Sarah Strohmeyer, Nancy Kress, Catherine Ryan Hyde, Lisa Black, John

Berendt, Janet Fitch, Lisa Jewell, and numerous other major and minor names in the professional writing, and entertainment world. I've garnered more than 1,600 new likes for my author page, I've made some new literary friends, I've had four promises of free book reviews in public forums, I've been slotted for two radio programs, and I've learned a ton. I received a purchase order for a block of my books from a local business, and had a tentative offer from another.

I've also offered my first book, 'Terminal Beginning' up for free to anyone who agrees to share a post, and like the page. The hope is that by giving something, I'll get what I need in return, and possibly develop new readership for later books.

How else did I work the guerrilla angles?

Here's what I did:

I began by friending a big-name author, whose work I enjoy. Then, I checked to see whom he knew that I might also be able to do so with. The first friending 'took', I'm guessing, because I had recently worked hard to assist in bolstering a Los Angeles bricks-and-mortar bookstore's business via their once floundering group page (whose owners are in my 'friends' list, and who are well known in many author circles). I did so much work, in fact, that they made me an admin of the page, even though I've never set foot in the place. Still, I conversed digitally with the owners, and the page manager, and got to know them. I had given something of value. I was rewarded for doing so in a way that I had never expected. I never intended to do anything more than to offer genuine help to a store that I enjoyed shopping online with. I did so with the expectation of receiving nothing in return but a good feeling for having done so.

This initial friending led to finding other New York Times, USA Today, and Amazon.com bestselling authors, who permitted me into their inner circles as well. As the list grew, I began to branch out, asking for friendship from the most likely candidates at each juncture. I couldn't believe it, but it worked.

I also made sure to thank them for adding me. Then, I've been waiting a day or two (or more, if their station in the literary world is high enough) to invite them to 'like' my author page.

During that weekend, I also went into my local city, and dropped off some 'samples' of my books, gratis, to business owners whom I wished to carry the books in their venues.

So, as stated above - I went from a 'nobody' author, to an author who is now on the radar of all of these fine folks. I intend to nurture these relationships (one of the predominant ways is having offered a number of them assistance in my computer support group page on Facebook, where all have received solutions, and to where some have even returned of their own volition (even inviting others, turning some of their friends on to the page as well). Now, they begin to know who I am. I am no longer a faceless fan, because I did the work, and interacted with them. I am now a helpful facet of their lives.

It's been hard, time consuming work writing so much product (read: books and blog entries), developing my editing skills, learning how to design and layout books and covers, all on my own.

But you know what?

Each one gets easier. God willing, all of this 'work' will lead me to my goal of being a paid writer in my early retirement. I could just as easily have sat around, waiting for someone to notice who I am. Instead, I worked my butt off to do the opposite.

And that friends is what guerrilla marketing, and guerrilla self-branding, are all about.

Now, think about this: how can *you* apply this sort of networking to your own business?

Come up with some ideas, start doing the work, and be diligent about it. Because if you don't, there is always someone else that will. And you'll never reach that next level if you don't try.

Review Your Way To Fame! (All Right - Maybe That's An Over-Sell)

Many bookseller websites allow you to write reviews of books.

Did you know that?

"So what?

Who cares?

Are you high when you write this stuff?

Because, I've got to tell you, you don't seem at all normal," you might say.

Well, what if you've purchased books from them?

Most likely, they are books about things that interest you, or that you enjoy. Once the book is read, take advantage of these stars aligning around you and write a review. Now here's the spin: within the review, find a way to tie it back to you, or the product or service you offer. Now you've offered a viable opinion and, if done well and in an interesting and concise manner, you might even get folks you don't even know interested in what you've written.

Have you been buying books on-line for years?

Many on-line providers have a 'purchase history' area. Use it. Review every book that you've ever purchased there (and read, of course) - all of them.

Further, many other sites that offer other products for sale allow similar review possibilities. Take into consideration the possible upsides, and review, review, review.

As a marketing tool, it's a bit of a stretch. That being said, it is one more way to get yourself noticed by readers of said reviews – with zero cost to you.

Turn Your Weekly Trash Experience Into An Opportunity

Would you be surprised to learn that, on 104 weekdays per year, you were missing an advertising opportunity?

It's true!

Let's talk for a minute about your garbage cans.

All right, is everyone done rolling their eyes and saying, *'Ewwww!'*?

Okay then... what?

No, Weird Uncle Pete, this is most certainly *not* a fetish post.

Don't you have somewhere else to be just now?

>AHEM<

As I was saying: your garbage cans are, potentially, blank slates for advertising. For those of you who do not provide your own receptacles, then you're out of luck, here. But for folks like me who do – keep reading!

What if you took them and spruced them up; made them into showpieces; a visual statement begging for eyeballs, defying those eyeballs *not* to look?

Sure it's kind of odd. I'm guessing, oddity aside, that you could work a slogan into the mix to alleviate some of the gross, and move the needle on the meter closer to the 'clever' range.

How?

How about something like this:

"If what you're buying now ends up here, then you're not buying the right stuff!"

Who wouldn't laugh (or take a picture, etc.) if they saw that?

So try it!

All it costs is some paint, creativity, and an hour or two.

Make Yourself A Marketing Ripple Effect

You've done it! You've arranged a meeting with a new client, and you're on your way!

Congratulations!

Hold on, though – do you have your personal, mobile advertising unit with you?

What?

You don't!?

Why not spruce up a blah briefcase, bland jacket, or boring bag, with your company logo. All the time you spend in your customer's facility is an opportunity to market to others. In fact, you're essentially sending the message to the folks around you at any given moment that, "This business uses my products or services! And you like this business, or you wouldn't be here. Therefore, vicariously, you should also use my services or products!"

Even if the business meeting doesn't have a happy ending, you've still set up other potential chapters to be written at a later date. So make the most of those meetings.

"Number Ten..."

David Letterman was funny. Okay, not all the time. And, to be fair, it was probably his writers who were due a goodly share of the credit, for good or ill. Still, he was funny.

If you ever watched his show (and I'm guessing that you have, at least once) then you know all about his staple, '*Top Ten*' lists. Now, I'll grant you that, at times, they were pretty lame. Sometimes, though, they made the leap from 'lame' to 'brilliantly funny'. This is where our focus lies.

Weird Uncle Pete?

Yes, come on over here, away from the poodles. Pay attention, now.

Maybe you need a '*Top Ten*' list of your own. One you can print out and leave places, give to potential customers, or post on your web site. And if you want it to stick or – better still – go viral, it needs to be *good*. Really, *really*, good.

So how do you take an individual (that's you) and make them hilarious (like I believe I am, regardless of the social outpouring negating that fact)?

You work at it. You painstakingly craft the humor.

Let's start at the beginning.

What makes your product or service superior?

What makes yours stand out among all of the others on offer?

What makes you different?

Make lists. Several, if need be. These will be your 'jumping-off' points. When you're done, choose the ten most poignant; the most important ones. These have now achieved list-worthy status.

So now you have your list. We just need to bring the funny to the table. Take each item in turn. If you get stuck, come back to it. A truly humorous endeavor like this can, believe it or not, take hours or even days to develop. Being funny is often difficult if you didn't grow up fat, like I did.

Let's create an example. I'm selling, '*Weird Uncle Pete's Smooth-As-Silk Sock Garters*'. It's a terrible product that (probably) no one wants, so it's a distinct challenge. One of the hypothetical selling points will be that they don't chafe, like those other sock garter brands do. Again – droll and extremely product-specific. We're still going to make it funny. For illustration purposes, I'll make an assumption. This product caters to older men on the go. It may not be true, but I need a focus for my humor – sort of a 'humor bulls-eye' to shoot for. And, just so you know, I'm creating these hypothetical situations immediately out of my head, to pose for myself a challenge, much like the one you will be faced with. Here's how we make it funny:

"Doesn't chafe like those other brands – or your in-laws."

Is it hilarious?
Not really, no. But we're at least on the road to funny. And this is just off the cuff.
What else can we do with this single premise?
Here are some other examples, some not so 'G' rated:

"The only chafing sensation you'll feel when wearing our garters is the one from the lap-dancing stripper."

"Any chafing sensation that you feel will be due to the male enhancement pills you took – not our garters."

"Chafes less than your trophy wife's butchering of the English language."

And this is all in a two-minute span.
Imagine if I weren't so lazy?
So get cracking, get a list, and most important of all get funny.

Make Your Next Trip To The Bathroom A Rosy One

Bathrooms: almost every place has one. Surprisingly, most also allow the public to use them. This is damn near to saintly, when you bear witness to the aftermath of *that* particular equation. Still, filthy or not, there's opportunity there. More so for men than women because – well – we can stand up and pee, and we always appreciate something to look at besides our tonkers while doing so.
Except for Weird Uncle Pete - he's usually checking out the... you know what?
Never mind.
Anyway, back to what I was saying.
Why not create a business-card-sized sign, preferably a single-fold

jobbie that is self-supporting, and could be left on top of the urinals?

You could put something catchy on it, a small ad, or a coupon that encouraged the urinal user to take it with them: anything.

For the women's bathroom, it becomes a little tougher. Based on the design and surroundings, I recommend trying to use the top of the toilet paper dispenser as your 'ground zero'. It's not as good as the urinal thing, but it also gives women something to look at while they're hovering and holding their noses. For this to work, you might consider taping a penny to the inside of one of the faces so the wind - either from the door closing and opening, or from 'other sources' - doesn't knock it down.

Or, if you have the means, how about magnetic business cards, for the back of the stall doors?

Will it work?

Who knows?

Only you, knowing your particular business, can be the judge of that. Just remember: everybody poops.

Do Disturb

Caution: what I'm about to suggest is probably frowned upon. So do it at your own peril. I'm not bailing you out if you do something dumb. Mostly, because they know me down there at the police station.

(Thanks again for *that*, Weird Uncle Pete!)

And now: the idea. Many larger towns and cities have hotels. And, no, I don't mean the *'No-Tell Motel'*, by the hour, touting their featuring of genuine color TV, types. I mean the large, often chain affiliated, ones. Yep – those bad boys.

To make money, local prefectures will often play host to specific groups, who all need a place to sleep (and sometimes, rut - I'm not here to judge, but I'm looking your way, Furries) in between their meeting, activities, conventions, etc. This is where you come in. Find out who's coming, and what they're into. Then figure out how to work it into a viable market for your product. If you can't, then at least you tried. If you can, then you're ready for step 2.

Step two: make, or have made, custom door hangers for the hotel rooms.

Not sure which rooms are theirs?

This is where what hackers call 'social engineering' comes in. Call the hotel, and find a clever way to ask what block of rooms is playing host to the event. If you sound nervous, or stupid, it won't work. You have to be confident. Pretend that you've never LARP'd before, and that don't know who Gary Gygax was, and you'll be fine.

If you can make it beyond that particular hurdle (without rolling a d12 with cold bonus), you are now faced with a new challenge: putting said hangers on said doors. Ultimately, anyone can (usually) walk into or out of a hotel, unmolested (unless the Furries are in town). The often-underpaid clerk might have a phenomenal memory, but unless he's Rain Man, he won't remember every face on every day. It's also important to point out that when you do something stupid, that's when you garner attention and get tossed out on your rear or – worse – get thrown in the pokey. So you need to do your deed, and be gone before someone takes the time to watch those video monitors and see that you're blanketing their establishment with advertising. Most likely, they'll assume you're on the coordinating committee for the visiting group, and not mind what you're doing because it's an interruption they don't get paid enough to bother with.

You should also consider – and implement – other methods of guerrilla delivery to your targeted audience. You know where they are, you know who they are, so go nuts and find clever ways to reach them while they're in town.

But, DO NOT BREAK THE LAW!

Refresh The Public - And Your Business

Here's a cheap and easy summer idea. For those of you rolling your eyes because it's November and there's eleven inches of powder outside, I apologize, but also say again: I can't control when you read this. My brain is a scary place. Not as scary as Weird Uncle Pete's is, mind you (it's a veritable horror show in there). Even so, while scary, it does not come complete with psychic abilities.

Yet.

If you live near a busy bike path, like I do, how about setting up a free, cold-water stand alongside it?

You could purchase some inexpensive cups, and either have gallons of water on ice in a cooler, or you could bring a 5-gallon, refrigerated, cooler with you (if you had a car cigarette lighter and could park next to the path). There are myriad twists on this idea that would work, so I'll leave you to work out the specifics. I highly recommend a partner in this endeavor, because some bike paths are also trolling grounds for ne'er-do-wells.

Or how about a free *Popsicle* stand?

You could purchase some bulk packs of those unnaturally colored, tubular popsicles and hand them out to passers-by from behind an advertising sign or table. Encouraging them, of course, not to litter when they're done!

Stick around for several hours with your company information (i.e. – *'This stand brought to you by the friendly folks at >Your Company Name*

Here<!') front and center (and more handy, should someone want a card!), and see how many parched friends you make.

Make A Public Spectacle Of Yourself

Recently, I was at a regional sporting event. Specifically, a hockey game, if you must know.

Jeez, you're nosey. And it's not like we're even dating.

Anyway: hockey game. Two beers, and one period down, I found myself visually exploring my surroundings during a break in play. The *Jumbo-Vision*-thingie came to life with real-time pictures of folks being wacky, dancing, etc. In fact, the more they shook their moneymakers, the more the cameras took notice and zoomed on in on them.

This phenomenon got me thinking: is there a way to capitalize on all of those eyeballs?

Scratch that – all of those *free* eyeballs?

Of course there is!

How?

Here are a couple of ideas:

If you have t-shirts that are legible, why not wear one to the game?

It not only makes sense, because of all those good fans who will see it while you're walking around (if even for the briefest of moments), but also because you could potentially get it on the big screen.

Want more?

What if you made a sign, something like: '*Digital Ninjas Media* Loves #42!*'

*(I have no idea who – if anyone – that is. It's just an example for the purposes of supposition. If you're #42, then please do not consider the above a tacit, requite-able, romantic invitation.)

Use your imagination, and have fun advertising while you're enjoying the game!

Your Credit Card: Marketing Everywhere You Want To Be

Credit Cards: they're everywhere. And they come in all flavors: Silver, Gold, Platinum, Titanium, Iridium, Polonium, Plum, Harpy, Platypus, and on and on. To me, it's a big bunch of insane nothingness perpetrated on the populace in an effort to make them feel better than someone else based solely on the color of a piece of plastic they wield, often to their own detriment. But, hey, that's just my opinion.

What do I know about psychology?

All right, back on topic. Some credit card companies allow you to 'customize' what's on the face of the card. It's an overt, yet significant, way for you to feel like you're in control. And for most, that's the place they want to be, even if it's only achieved via a cursory feeling.

Most folks choose to put something important to them on it: little Frank's t-ball picture, a favorite piece of artwork, or poodles mating (in the case of Weird Uncle Pete). As a business owner this is an opportunity for you to put a conversation starter on the card. Make it pop. If you've got something on there that can somehow tie back to your business *and* get the attention of the cashier, then you've just completed a marketing circuit.

It's a small victory, I'll grant you. But it's one that's simple to achieve.

Mail Call!

Your mailbox: For the most part, it's a utilitarian necessity that goes largely unnoticed. At least, most do.

But have you ever seen the ones that look like trucks?

Fishing lures?

Sports helmets?

Animals?

Two rhinos playing badminton?

If you have, you *remember* that you have because *those* mailboxes were *interesting*.

See where I'm going with this?

First – and I do mean numero uno – find out what national, state, and local postal requirements for mailboxes in your area are in place. And ABIDE BY THEM. I won't tolerate breaking the law, nor be the catalyst for it. You've been warned.

Need I bring the nun analogy back into play?

>Looking behind myself<

There we go. I think my hynie is covered.

You know what?

I just realized that I have no notion of what the proper spelling of 'hynie' is.

Weird. Now, back to the mailbox situation:

Think about what it is that you sell, or do. How can you incorporate that into a stunning, informational mailbox?

I'm not saying it will be easy – it won't. And it helps if you have a gifted child, family member, or friend who works for video games, beer, or the pleasure of your company, to assist in making the thing pop.

Get Your Business Band! (Pun *Totally* Intended)

Have a band?

No?

Know someone who does?

No?

Okay then, think about how unlucky you are while I proselytize to the rest of the good folks reading this.

All right, those of you who are still with me on this: are you in a band, or do you know someone who is?

How much do they love you, and how talented are they?

Why?

Because both are about to come into play with what I'm about to suggest.

Write a song. Write a song about your business that is either highly catchy and memorable or (easier still) funny or self-deprecating. Then record it. Amateur recording is fine, in this instance, but semi-professional would be the Holy Grail.

Once complete, you may (at the very least) either hand out CD's of the song in your store, to your clients with your business card, etc. Or, what I would suggest, is that you can post it on-line, on your web site, *Facebook* page, *YouTube* channel, etc. If it's good enough, it will make its own way into the world.

If not?

Well, then, all you're out is some beer and cookies from when you fed the band. Unless you let one of them stay on your couch for a 'few days' while he and his 'old lady' patch things up. Then, you're screwed, and I'm not helping you get rid of the freeloader who now receives mail at your place.

If you're *really* ambitious, and have a *really* talented group, you can make an entire 'concept album' on the subject.

What's a 'concept album'?

Think *The Who*'s 'Tommy', *Pink Floyd*'s 'The Wall', or *Boston*'s 'Third Stage'. Those are all good examples (and amazing albums, as well).

Kill Your Spare Time Creatively

Have some spare time?

Too much spare time, perhaps?

Do you like to write?

Do you have an opinion?

Congratulations!

I have a weird marketing idea for you!

Let's assume that you have a great deal of time on layovers, in waiting rooms, hotels – whatever. Often, you can make good use of that time – do that first. But if you have more time left over, then this will give you a new and free marketing outlet.

Many printed publications (newspapers, newsletters, magazines, specialty publications, and on and on) have an open forum that allows readers to submit ideas, thoughts, comments, etc.

The only requirement?

It has to be relevant, and it has to be read by you to know that the option is there.

So you, as a newly minted potential contributor, do the following:

- Check the publications you already receive for this option
- Inform everyone you know what you're up to, and have them look for opportunities for you. It could be as simple as them calling you with the meat of the article and an address. Voila – you can now be a contributor.
- Flip through all of those waiting room magazines. And, if possible, check out what *Goofus & Gallant* are up to these days.
- Be prepared to be creative

Once you find something that you can make a legitimate contribution to, begin crafting the letter or submission. Make it clear, concise, and above all relevant and poignant. This will allow you the best opportunity for publication. The trickiest part is working your business in to the body of the piece.

Send it off, and wait. Keep checking the column/area and hope they publish you.

Now, let's assume that they have.

Congratulations!

You just hit a bunch of new eyeballs!

But we're not done with your newfound sliver of fame. You may now check to see if a digital version of the publication is available. If it is, then you can link to the commentary on your web site or *Facebook* page. It adds some depth and interest that you didn't have before.

If they don't offer it in digital format that's okay!

Scan the article, and if you have the ability, the cover, and create a digitized graphic of the whole work so as to – again – publish your contribution*.

*(Just don't break any copyright laws!)

It's a simple, but time-consuming way to practice your writing skills, get noticed, and seem like you're that much better than you were yesterday.

Build Your Own Little Marketing Kingdom

As we've developed our business, lo these many years now, I've noticed numerous trends in the local mercantile community. One I began to see was that many of the businesses whose ear I had bent successfully were reliant on well-advertised and hosted fairs, shows, etc. to market and sell their wares.

So I started paying further attention. Specifically to who these individuals were, what they were selling, and where they were selling it. Over the week that I did this, an idea began to form.

I thought, *'Why can't Digital Ninjas Media, Inc. sponsor an event like this?'*

The answer was: there's no reason that we can't.

A second question then bubbled to the surface, *'Okay, then why would we want to?'*

This one required a far less glib answer.

On one hand, I considered the fact that we could charge the obligatory 'entry fee' for the vendors. Sometimes, an entry fee is also required at the door for incoming patrons.

Here's the thing, though: I didn't really want to charge the vendors a participation/space fee. And I *really* didn't want to charge the potential customers an entry fee.

Then how to 'sponsor' the event?

If we were going to do this, we had to get *something* out of it. Preferably free positive advertising, while at least breaking even.

Why am I sharing this with you?

Because the more I considered the whole fair/vendor concept, the more I realized that it's a crucial piece of supporting local, cottage and small businesses. And it's something that you could be a part of, as an event sponsor – using some, all, or none of the following ideas.

Here's a few that I came up with:

Potential Benefit #1:

Allow vendors who are participating in your circles (i.e. – 'Likers', 'Followers', 'Subscribers', etc.) get first crack, and the best spots. If you market the event correctly, you could stipulate that ONLY these folks could participate.

Guess how much your following will grow?

Potential Benefit #2:

Allow anyone who asks to participate, so long as there are no conflicts in vendors (i.e. – only one rep from *Scentsy, Pampered Chef, Lia Sophia,* etc.). Still allow your throng first crack – you owe them that much. Don't charge to enter the show, nor to exhibit. Instead, ask for a percentage of profits earned. This requires an honor system, but it also shows how kind and trusting you can be. Someone will most likely take advantage of this – expect it. But that's not your primary concern, here. Marketing is. Making a few bucks is secondary.

Potential Benefit #3:
Name the show/fair in a way that ties back to your business. This, I admit, could be tough – or downright impossible. But if it can be done, all the publicity for the event will have your name in it. And this is a great marketing coup.

8

Potential Benefit #4:
Your throng is not comprised of hermit island dwellers. They have friends, relatives, and business contacts. And word of this insane plan will get out, sooner or later - *your* plan. You're the guy (or gal) who made this crazy thing happen. This will cause immediate (and continuing/residual) exposure for you, and your business enterprise. Ideally this will result in new clients, or new throng members who you may now court as potential clients.

I don't know. All of this 'thinking out loud' might be insane.
Weird Uncle Pete, would you care to weigh in on this?
No?
Oh, *now* he shuts up.
All right, fine.
Somehow, somewhere, someone is going to find a way to make this work and do it. I don't know when, and I don't know how, but it's a thought experiment that I find that I, personally, just cannot walk away from without sharing.

A High-Flying Idea
It's been a few pages since I've offered up a potentially stupid-crazy idea, so I figured it was about time again.
Ready?
Did you know that in many areas there are companies that offer aerial advertising?
It's true!
Before we began our business, I spent days developing an internal web page, with organized links to all sorts of advertising outlets. I did so as a potential free reference tool to be provided to our clients. On a whim, I decided to see if this sort of advertising was available in our area. I was fairly surprised to find that it is.
What does this mean to you?
It means that you can pay someone to fly a plane around the area, trailing your customized business message.

My suggestion?

Do it on a major festival weekend, when lots of folks are outdoors. All those eyeballs will be exponentially drawn to that sign in the sky because, hey – we're all curious – even if we have imbibed copious amounts of beer and/or other adult beverages.

Happy Birthday! Let's Both Receive A Present!

Everyone has a birthday (whether they own up to that fact anymore well, that's another story). Since 'everyone' also includes your clientele, let's consider giving you both a gift for their birthday. Here's what I mean:

When I was sixteen, I worked for a brief time in a comic book store. This store also sold games, books, and anything else that often accompanies such things. It was here, that I had the opportunity to work with a very savvy businessman as an employer. Unfortunately, I'm also savvy, and our collective savvy didn't gel too well. To be fair to him, I was sixteen, and more cocky than I should have been. This particular employer, however, was a genius when it came to getting bodies in the door, and cash in the registers. To be frank, I still admire a number of his business strategies. One of which has stuck with me for decades. It was called '*The Birthday Club*'.

The Birthday Club functioned thusly: when a customer checked out, they were asked if they were a member of *The Birthday Club*. When we started doing this, of course, no one was. But the tactic was to immediately inquire as though it were something that had been there for some time, and that they had, somehow, just missed being a part of up until that moment.

If they said no, then we asked if they would like to become one.

If they said yes, then we moved on to the signup phase. As far as the 'no's' went, they usually followed up with an astute inquiry of their own.

"What is *The Birthday Club*?"

Occasionally, I also got, "Where's the john?" and "What business is it of yours?"

We'll focus less on the latter (read: not at all), in this particular case, and more on the parties open to membership.

The Birthday Club began with a form. It required a name, address, and birth date. It also allowed the customer to choose any of a number of extremely precise check boxes of the things in the store that they typically purchased, or were interested in. Finally, it offered them a place for their own thoughts, ideas, and suggestions.

What we received over the months, and subsequent years, was a deluge of information. We knew what percentage of our customers liked 'X' product, which ones liked 'Y', and so on. We learned which areas of the store were ripe for expansion, or due for contraction. We also learned about new things to carry in everyday stock (rather than special order, which we also gladly accommodated), based on their suggestions.

When it came time for a sale in the store, we targeted customers on their personal interest categories via mail. We could also gain a concise awareness of what neighborhoods these folks were predominantly from, to hang on to, should we ever choose to employ it.

"But what did they receive, in return for all of this awesome data?" you might ask.

They received a letter, two weeks prior to their birthday. By presenting this letter for forfeiture during a transaction in the store, they were afforded a 15% discount on anything they bought – sale and clearance items *included*. We wanted it to be straightforward.

On the surface, this seems a little crazy. But here's what's REALLY crazy: A customer who would normally make a $10.00 purchase now made a $100.00 purchase. And the $100.00 regulars would often break the four-digit barrier without blinking an eye. High-dollar items that tended to languish would disappear during these binges, and in the end we ended up making more profit – dollar wise – on their visit than we would have on their normal ones. Sometimes, folks would even bring along a cousin, or friend, and buy stuff on their behalf with the letter within the same transaction. And we let them, because while it meant a leaner margin, it also meant more raw dollars in product moved.

It also got customers in the door (possibly for the one time per year that they would do so) to see new inventory, changes in the store, etc. This often resulted in more 'dropping by' so as not to miss anything, as each year progressed. More often than not, everyone left the store having bought something.

For these reasons, and more, this was why it was such a resounding success. The owner elected to eliminate all the strings attached, in return for information that was exceedingly useful to him. In this day and age, it would be an even more useful tool.

Why?

Because with the advent of e-mail, you'd save on stamps, could broadcast to an e-mailing list about sales and events, and on and on. The customer would gladly allow this intrusion because their participation in the club demanded it, and there was no way they were going to give up that sizable discount on anything, once a year, in lieu of the small inconvenience of receiving an e-mail once in a while.

Of course, this idea worked very well for the business model it was used in. Your business model may not be applicable to this precise formulation of the idea. But if you take the time to consider it within the constraints that your business model poses, I can't help but think that you could come up with a silver bullet version of your own.

So I ask you again: Are you a member of *The Birthday Club*?

In Three... >Two<... >One<...

Public Access Television programs - we've all seen them, usually as we surf around at four am looking for something that isn't an infomercial or home shopping to watch.

If you haven't, then... well... pretend that you have, all right?

So how did those folks get on your television at four am, anyway?

Is this where all of those alien abductees go during their 'lost time'?

In order for this to work, one or more of your local television stations needs to offer public access. If they do not, then you're excused from this segment.

If they do, it will be imperative to discuss the restrictions, rules, regulations, and specifics with a station representative to discover whether or not you have an idea for a program that meets their criteria.

If you pass muster on this front, you've only just begun. Now you have to develop an informative, interesting, and compelling program for the public at large to see. I would also recommend publicizing the bajeebers out of your upcoming endeavor on your website, social media outlets, and within your physical store or show space. Maybe even provide reminder cards, or e-mails to your followers. Ideally, you have a few viewers who tell their friends after the first outing is complete and they, in turn, tune in the next time.

Which brings up another point: if you're only interested in doing a one-off that's fine. But it won't be anywhere near as successful as a serial program.

Plan accordingly, and well in advance, of any advertising that you do.

Whatever it is, be creative!

Most television is simple-minded pabulum aimed at the lowest common denominator in a flurry of boobs and guns. This is okay, I guess, if this is your niche market.

Me? In case you haven't noticed, I like humor. Laughter, to me, is an equalizing force amongst all races and peoples. Getting a few chuckles out of someone, while being informative or interesting (in my opinion) leaves a far more lasting impression than the alternatives.

So go forth, prepare, educate and dazzle!

What have you got to lose?

Part 3: The Tried & The True (With Some New Twists)

Do Your Homework To Find The Cool Kids,
Even If They're Not In Your Area

Chambers of Commerce are a great way to get your business instantly recognized in your locale. For what is (usually) a nominal fee, you become a member and - to me - the real benefit of membership lies in the ability to access a group of like-minded individuals without having to 'build up' the base of them over several years on your own.

Most CoC's also offer the option of having a ribbon cutting ceremony. This is, at its essence, a public 'coming out' for your business. Often, the media will cover the event or, at the very least, make mention of it.

As a member, you will also be afforded access to unique benefits offered to the collective that may not otherwise be available to a cottage or small business. These often come in the form of discounts, advice, advertising specials, and any number of other myriad, useful things.

Chambers of Commerce are also notorious for hosting 'mingle events', where members, and potential members, are invited to get together for a predetermined excuse and spend a morning/afternoon/evening, usually eating, drinking, golfing - or all three - and commiserating with one another. These events can be great ways to meet new individuals and promote your business. You may also find individuals doing likewise, who may offer you a special rate on a useful product or service.

One mistake I find many businesses making (aside from not looking into joining these organizations at all) is either joining them, and then forgetting about them, or joining them, and then joining others as well. There are several problems with both of these. First and foremost, if you spend the money to join, but interact no further with the organization, then you've essentially bought yourself an expensive and ineffectual advertisement in the form of a 'new member' blurb in the limited distribution channels of the CoC's newsletter. Secondly, if you join too many at once, you won't be able to successfully cultivate the relationships that these organizations afford, because you'll be spread too thin to effectively attend the events that you need to be mingling at. So choose one - and choose wisely - to start.

Speaking on this point, when I researched CoC's for our business, I looked not only in our immediate area, but in our surrounding area as well. You may not be aware, but most Chambers of Commerce will allow you to join their organization whether your physical location is found in their city/town/zip code/realm or not. What I found through my research was that the locale that I'm in has a very weak 'good-old-boy'-ish chamber of commerce. In speaking with other members of the business community, I found that my money would be better spent joining the neighboring community's CoC. In the end, this is what I did. I avoided what could have been a potential low rate of return and traded it for a higher one by doing nothing more than a little homework.

A second thing that I found dumbfounding was the wildly varying joining fees, versus the benefits offered. A small town on the outskirts of my area had, by far, the most lopsided ratio I found anywhere. After some research, I could find no reason for this. Suffice it to say, I did not join that CoC.

In closing, don't let me dissuade you completely from joining more than one CoC. I would merely encourage you to cultivate one - from planting the seeds to harvesting the rewards - before moving on to the next. And remember: members come and go. Businesses sprout up and fail. It's a fact of the business world. What this means to you is an ever-rotating crop of potential clients/customers just waiting to be harvested.

If nothing else remember this: you get what you give. If you make efforts to get to know these individuals, not just as fellow business owners, but as individual persons as well, then you should expect reciprocal circumstances to present themselves. Conversely, if you do nothing, then don't expect anything in return. Joining a CoC is work. The difference is that it can be a much different (and much more enjoyable) form of it.

Survey Says!

The survey: you've all seen them. Perhaps you've even participated in a few.

For the most part, here is my advice: forget everything you've ever seen about surveys, because - in my opinion - they're often ineffectual and designed incorrectly.

I'm pretty sure that got a few eyebrows raised. If not, then go have your coffee and come back. I can wait, and I know it might be early (depending upon when you're reading this).

...

Okay, caffeinated now? All right then, here we go:

For whatever reason, most surveys like to focus on the experience of the individual. This is a good thing. Where it starts to go bad is when number scales and feel-good questions are included. These are, typically, bad things masked as mainstream good ideas. I'll put my helmet on now, so you can throw things in disagreement. Please, though: no poodles.

Let's start by deconstructing the number scale. It's arbitrary, its usefulness is difficult to quantify, and if you don't ask the exact, right, precise question, it's worthless. I can't tell you how many times I have filled out one of these number-scale based surveys, only to come to the end and find that *my* needs weren't being met, and that it ended up seeming like I was happier than I really was.

The result?

That just makes me cranky (more than usual, even).

My next gripe is with the 'feel good' questions. If you want people to tell you how amazing you are, then you probably shouldn't stick it in their face to get that feedback. It's narcissistic, and sort of self-aggrandizing (like me!)

Imagine if you're at a holiday gathering with the family, and Weird Uncle Pete does nothing but come up to everyone and say, "How awesome am I, on a scale from one to eleven?!" only to leave once all have been questioned. You'd never intentionally invite him back, especially with his known proclivity for poodles.

About a decade ago, I had a long discussion with my then-boss about a survey that I intended to launch on the company's behalf to all of our existing customer's buyers, as well as our tier-one vendors. I was coloring outside the lines and I think that, at first, the concept seemed ridiculous to him. I could see his point, to some degree. He had been weaned on those surveys that I've been bitching about. I myself, as a child of the *MTV* generation, and a person who knows what I hate when I see it, chose to persevere on this point that I felt so strongly about. In the end he acquiesced. Though I can't say for certain how sure he truly was about the whole affair. It's a testament to either his faith in me, or his desire to have me just go away and stop being a burr under his saddle. Either one could be germane, in this case.

What I proposed was this: a survey that began with the statement, *"We'd like to think we know what we're doing right. What we need from you is the unabashed truth about what we're doing WRONG. Where are we failing, and how can we serve your specific needs better?"*

I elected to make the survey anonymous, so that the recipients could come at me, both barrels blazing. I included some leading questions about things we might be doing wrong (specifically, generalized areas of business).

At the end, I provided this final statement: *"If you feel like you're beating us up – don't. Your honesty is the single biggest favor that you can bestow upon us."*

You won't believe what happened: I got responses. Not a great many, but genuine responses that I could use to tweak my business practices. For example:

I found that one of our Canadian clients hated hand written quotes, and felt that we took way too long to return them to him. This was news to us, as we do all of our quotes within hours of receipt. We tracked that problem to its end, and found it was a server issue on his end. We also changed the quote format to the one he preferred.

He tackled the server problem on his end and – voila! – happy customer.

In fact, he took the time to write us a short thank you letter. It stated that he had never seen a survey like that, nor felt that he had been heard so resoundingly, and taken so seriously.

This was big win #1.

There were several others, all unique to individual buyers all across the United States and Canada. By the time we were done chasing all of the issues down, we had received several such personal messages like the one above.

Want to know the most interesting part?

Nowhere on the survey did we even remotely ask for praise in any way, shape, form, or kind: NOWHERE. Yet, numerous customers took the time to add their own praise at the bottom, or in attached letters. They went out of their way to make sure we knew how they felt about the positives. That is the sort of feedback that really means something.

So consider all of these things the next time you sit down to develop a survey. Focus on what your goals really are, and don't open yourself up to praise. It might be the single best survey you've ever done, and the results will mean a whole lot more.

Why You Need A Blog

Since 1992, in one form or another, I've had a web site. The form it takes today is a far cry from the monstrous nightmare that most of us had back then (i.e. - they were basically a big sheet of paper with links, pictures, and God-awful animated icons and backgrounds.) The web site that my wife and I share today (www.heathnwanda.com) is a simplistic, raw-coded, amalgam of stuff we find useful. It's written for us first, and public consumption second, mostly because when we put it up in its current form, what seems like ages ago, we were nobodies who wanted to keep our HTML coding skills sharp.

Nearly two decades (and far better HTML software) later, we've elected to simply leave it be, as we've moved on to other things. One thing, in particular, that I left alone against reason, logic, better judgment, and the chiding of numerous friends was my blog. My blog is still written in raw HTML code, with no interactivity (though, I haven't added new entries in years, now).

Why would I choose this?

I don't know, exactly. It just felt right for me. When I began the blog in

2006, I did so as a method of preserving the more interesting high points in my life. It's amazing how much you imagine you won't forget, and how insignificant it seems when you make and post an entry. Yet, years later, most of the stories I relive through it are otherwise long forgotten, and, sometimes they have a much deeper and more important meaning now.

This leads me to reason number one: for the sake of posterity, even in the face of Alzheimer's. There's no humor intended there, either. I watched as the brilliant mind of my Grandfather deteriorated to nothing via this insidious disease. This made me realize how amazing it would be to have all of my own memories (in blog form), even after I had physically lost them, should that day ever come to pass.

God willing, it won't.

Further, how amazing would it be for the remaining family, after your passing, to have a memoir of your life?

You might think it insignificant, but I'm guessing that Laura Ingalls-Wilder didn't begin her writing with the intention of publishing it someday. Without her now-significant works, we would have lost a high level of detailed insight into our collective heritage.

Reason number two, for me, is also important: it allows me to practice writing, even if no one reads it. My writing, while not stellar by any stretch of the imagination, has progressed markedly over the past ten years (five of which were spent actively blogging). I am more comfortable writing, and feel that I have a better handle on what works and what doesn't. My lexicon has also expanded.

With the advent of the opening of our media business, I knew that I had to bring something special to the table when it came to the blog(s) for the new web site. My wife developed and implemented three blogs (only two of which have actual writing) for me to have my way with (she's the web genius in the group, these days). One was developed for news and highlights to showcase business happenings. The other was meant to be 'found' by the public at large, and subscribed to for content. This one originally centered on Guerrilla Marketing, but sort of branched out, over time, into business management and practice as well.

While readership on the web is small, the same content was made available on *Facebook*, where readership was substantially higher.

The result?

I became 'the guy' for a lot of local business folks to send messages and e-mails to when they had questions they felt I could answer. To be honest, I was flattered, but I was also amazed at the level of candor and trust that these folks were imparting upon me. It was - and continues to be - a truly gratifying and humbling experience.

The above story segues nicely into reason number three: to become a publicly recognized, de-facto leader in your field of experience and expertise, whatever it may be.

By offering those posts and entries to anyone who would listen, I became a touchstone for them. This was especially so in situations where their personal experience was either insufficient or non-existent. And I cannot tell you how many customers that one single blog led into the fold of our company. For the first three months of active business, we had more clients and projects than we ever dared hope for - all because of this one inlet.

Now, take a moment to consider what it is that you, and your business, do. How can you turn your day-to-day actions into something interesting? It might seem difficult at first (and sometimes, it truly is), but consider sharing some of the following:

- Problems that you've solved
- Insight based on personal experience
- Potential problems that you, or your customers, are facing
- Historic information surrounding your business, or facets of it
- Trivia or interesting facts
- Giveaways or contests
- Hints, tips, tricks, and workarounds
- Photos and descriptions of new products
- Useful information on existing products, or their production/makeup
- Calendar of events

I could honestly go on for pages, but hopefully by now you've got those creative juices flowing.

One other important point: make the content regular. It doesn't have to be daily, or even weekly (though at least weekly is my personal preference), but it also cannot be sporadic, or you risk losing readership at an alarming rate. If you choose to write a blog, commit to it for a period of time. Then, don't allow yourself to back out. You're in this for the duration, so fulfill that promise that you've made to yourself, as well as the unspoken one that you've made to your readership.

Have you decided that a blog may be right for you?

Great! (I'm assuming you said yes, because I'm feeling super-persuasive at the moment).

There are numerous sites available for budding bloggers that are free to use, and fairly intuitive. I recommend doing a web search, asking friends, and other business owners which ones they prefer - and why - to hone in on the one that's right for you.

In closing, remember this very, very important point: if you cannot write without butchering the English language, that's okay. What is not okay is letting your readership know this. I recommend writing in a program that offers spelling and grammar checks. Even after the fact, find a friend or relative to proofread the work before it goes live. No one wants to read something that looks foolish or clunky. So don't scare your potential readership away in this manner.

Who Are The People In Your Neighborhood?

Want more exposure in your neighborhood or town?

Use the age-old trick of the flyer. They're inexpensive to produce (a word processor, typewriter, scissors and glue, a copier, printer, or any combination work as well as fancy graphic arts for these). You can place them on mailboxes (but not in – they're not mail, and that's illegal!), in newspaper cubbies, and on doors. This may all be done while you and or your dog/cat/family take a stroll through the neighborhood.

Can't find the time?

Find a reputable young person looking to make a few extra dollars to do it. While you may not get a ton of response, the response that you do get should more than cover your costs and time. Hopefully, there's even room for some profit as well!

Remember: before just diving in, make sure that you contact your local officiating entity for your prefecture, and consult your subdivision covenants, to make certain that there are no ordinances or laws prohibiting your doing the above – obey the rules!

Music Sets The Mood

When I was sixteen, and still working my second job* at the sign of the big red K, I would go in to work each day to be greeted with the best that forty years of pop, soft rock, and country had to offer. Fortunately, I had spent a lot of my formative years experimenting with music. While most kids were listening to nothing, or pabulum, I would play with my parent's console stereo listening to their albums. These included *The Doors, Sly & The Family Stone, Three Dog Night, Simon & Garfunkel, Jim Croce*, and on and on. I learned from an early age to appreciate music. By the age of eight, my Grandfather had introduced me to classical music, so I gained an appreciation for Ravel, Mozart, Bach, Dvorak, and Chopin at a time when most kids couldn't spell their names.

*(I started working when I was twelve, in a wood shop owned by a family friend, until I could get a real job, in case you were wondering. There, I was exposed to the likes of *Jethro Tull, The Who, R.E.O. Speedwagon, Styx, Led Zeppelin*, and *Pink Floyd*.)

So where am I going with this?

Well, instead of tuning the music out, I listened. I would find myself hoping to hear a certain song, and would get a cheap thrill when it arrived over the satellite feed of 'The K-Mart Radio Network' (it was, in fact, called that). I learned a lot about those genres in those few years that I remained there.

I also found that many other places offered music to their shoppers. Borders Books brought me in touch with the band Pulp, Half-Price Books with Beth Orton, and a number of other places and songs began to mount up. Today, I have a collection of music that runs about 150,000 songs strong. I treasure them, and listen to music every day.

What does any of this have to do with your business?

I'm finally there!

Being young and inquisitive, I entered a conversation with one of the wizened managers in the K-Mart store about the concept of music within the confines. I was surprised (at the time) to learn that it was a psychological issue; that studies had been done. Apparently, some years ago, he had taken the time to avail himself of this knowledge via an article that he had read. Where, he could not then recall.

What he told me, however, was fascinating.

Specifically, he spouted some haphazardly recalled numbers about the average number of minutes folks spent in a store with, and without, music. I really wish that he could have recalled the specifics, though I'm sure that even if he had, I would not, now.

I did a little research, and in a nutshell, here's what I came up with:

In retail settings, there are two schools of thought: to play, or not to play, really popular songs. In the past, hits of yesteryear were chosen so as to give the shopper something familiar to listen to, but not too familiar. This is in contrast to some stores who choose to play top pop hits. This flies in the face of what the psychology once indicated. Specifically that it distracted the buyer from shopping, and random browsing, by making the song more prominent in their mind.

I agree with this line of thinking, mostly because I've had negative experiences while shopping to current pop 'hits' (I'm looking at you, Wal-Mart).

Music also has a similar effect on employee's work habits. If the music doesn't blend pleasantly into the background, they're more likely to focus on the music as well, leading to decreased productivity and job focus.

For my money?

I can see both schools of thought. But I'm still on board with the prior theory. The only potential exception is that folks may tend to see this as less 'trendy'. It's a trade-off.

Then, there's the classical music camp. Every time I visited a Barnes & Noble, I found myself immersed in the exquisite choices in classical fare on offer. I relaxed, I took my time, and I was fluid.

And you know what?

Studies have indicated that classical music provides a medium for shoppers to shop for a more protracted period of time, while also being more open to purchasing items of higher cost.

I personally concur, based solely on my own personal experiences.

Then again, a lot of folks think classical music is 'icky'. But, in the case above, those folks also won't tend to find themselves in the target demographic of that particular establishment. As such, it still makes sense to move forward with that music of choice.

And then, there's the groceteria (a word I made up [so far as I know], that I've been trying to get established for about fifteen years now. I'm still deluded enough to believe that it might happen). Grocery stores use slower-paced music in an effort to get patrons to move - and shop - more slowly. The slower the movement, the more time the eyes have to take in the offerings on the shelves. It's all about eyeball time. It's hard to recall that you *did* just run out of canola oil, if it isn't on your list. It's easier, if you're scanning the aisles and your eyes hit upon it. And studies have shown a whopping 38% increase in sales in grocery stores when slower music was applied to the patrons.

Own a restaurant?

If so, then you have the opposite problem. In the words of *Ed Debevic*, you want your customers to *'Eat it, then beat it.'* Table turnover is important to keep waits down, keep wait staff happy and well-tipped, and to promote the most revenue in your proverbial till at the end of each evening.

Part of the reason trendy restaurants are expensive (aside from the chefs, the quality foodstuffs provided, and the complex recipes) is that they're designed to be low-turnover. Part of that cost is built into the sometimes staggering price of said foodstuffs provided.

So, if you own a non-high-end restaurant, your best choice it to play fast-paced, energetic, music. This keeps the old juices a-flowin' in the patrons, making them less logy and lethargic. An energized patron is less likely to park his or her posterior in your precious booth or seat for too long.

The most important thing of all, regardless of what sort of establishment that you own, is to know your customer. Play music that meets both your needs, and theirs. And if you're a trendy, hip place to shop, make *really* certain that if you are playing something new, awesome, and obscure, that you consider having copies of the CD playing for sale. I can't tell you how often I've wanted to purchase what a store who actually sells CD's was playing, only to find that it was not for sale there. That's just dumb. Don't be dumb.

The Line Card: Kicking Your Competition's Butt Since The Gutenberg Press

Line cards - wait, what's that?

What do you mean 'you don't know what a line card is'?

Wait - seriously!?

How can you have lived this long and not... OUCH!

My wife just snipped my ear!

She also says, 'Don't be a jerk!'

Fine, fine - but she didn't have to snip my ear.

Let me start again.

A line card is a single-page, short, succinct, clearly and concisely formatted 'shopping list' or 'menu' of the products or services that you and your business offer to the world at large. A really good one will give the most information in the least amount of words. The great ones will even have comprehensible pricing structures included within the verbiage. Pictures are often a plus, but not always necessary (or relevant).

For our business, we had developed a line card before we even opened our doors. It's a great way to be able to permanently communicate what you have to offer to potential clients. It's also a cost-effective means of transferring the maximum amount of data in the smallest, and least likely to be disposed of, manner when networking or meeting potential clients on the fly.

They're useful to keep around at all times (because - hey - you just never know). When writing them, they're also a phenomenal exercise in paring your business down to its very essence. When it comes to an initial introduction to your business (in my humble opinion) less is more. If you hand me a quasi-catalog with 3-color glossy photographs with circles and arrows and a caption on the back*, I'm really unlikely to digest the whole thing. In fact, my initial instincts are usually to just toss the thing. And this is sad because I know - I *KNOW* - that I've missed opportunities to explore products or services that I truly need.

*(Thanks, Arlo Guthrie!)

Line cards are a different animal. By going minimal, they offer a 'big picture' in a small package, thereby allowing the customer to pursue follow-up interaction.

How do I know?

It happens to me - often. Specifically, my day job requires me to purchase tens of thousands of dollars in raw metals, tooling, and supplies each month. And while most are readily available, some of the more exotic metals are a real pain in the hind-end to get my hands on (especially at a reasonable price). So when a steel vendor walks in, I skim their line card.

What am I looking for?

Four things: 316 Stainless, 317 Stainless, 4150 Annealed, and 655 Bronze. If they have a line for those, I'm finding out more.

Why?

Because these are things that I actually need sources for.

For those vendors who walk in with a shiny folder full of magnets, gee-gaws and doo-dads, I usually distribute the freebies to whoever is handy and wants them, open the folder for two seconds, see it's a lot of stuff I don't have the time, nor desire, to read, and toss it.

While I may be in a minority, I still feel that I'm a good case study (did I mention that I'm also a narcissist?) Line cards tell me that the vendor knows my time is important. The fact that they've taken the time to allow me to peruse their offerings in a compact format appeals to me.

113

As you're reading this, you might be saying, "Heath, you don't know beans. A line card won't work for my business model!"

To which I would most likely reply, "I'm not a legumeologist," (probably not a real thing, anyway) and, "You're wrong."

In fact, one could potentially argue that the bare essence of your offerings would be more likely to afford you a second interaction with the potential customer.

Why?

Because if they see something there they are interested in pursuing, they will then contact you for more information, on their time or on their turf. Now THEY have come to YOU. Then it's your time to shine, and hopefully convert them into a customer.

So in summation: a line card is a short, succinct, 'menu' of your business' offerings. It may contain pricing - or it may not. Depending on your business model, either may be preferable. It should be an exercise in minimalism (and if you're bad at this, challenge yourself to write some haiku for a week, and then come back to it. I find that it's amazing what haiku can do for your writing acumen).

Above all else, keep it simple. Make it portable. Make it available at a moment's notice. And for the love of Weird Uncle Pete, be prepared to shine when the customer tracks you down and begins asking the questions.

Car Magnets & Their Significant Others

Car magnets are a convenient way to advertise your business while on the go. They can be removed when you want to go low-key, which for some is a bonus.

They can also be a pain. Over time, they can damage the vehicle (if left in place, and unremoved), kids love to steal them, and probably more stuff that I haven't considered and refuse to research, which I'll just admit is laziness.

Static decals, however, level the playing field to your advantage. You can now purchase 8 1/2" x 11" sheets of PRINTABLE (yep – you read that right!)

static-cling decals. These can be placed INSIDE of a vehicle, and they won't harm them a bit. Plus, you can create them in your own home, inexpensively, without hiring a third party you have to pay for the service.

And who wants to go to the trouble to steal THAT?

Better still: how about printing up a batch of them, and asking the kids, Mom, Dad, and Weird Uncle Pete to put them in their vehicles as well?

Perhaps offer them some incentive (cookies, free product or services, pictures of your poodle in compromising situations for Weird Uncle Pete).

A potential fleet of mobile billboards at minimal cost has just been mobilized.

Social Donations & Benevolent Marketing: Your Friends With Benefits

Today, we broach a subject that my Mother and I don't quite see eye-to-eye on: benevolent marketing.

In my community of friends and neighbors, I invariably find folks asking for donations for a benefit – usually cancer. And I can't sympathize enough with folks going through that, having known more than my fair share of individuals afflicted (some still with us, and some not, God rest their awesome souls). For cancer, I give what I can without a second thought.

For other things, I usually choose to offer something for the silent auction/raffle, in an effort to help out, but also – yes – gain something from it.

I'm pretty sure that my Mom is disowning me right about now.

I usually give some signed copies of my books, with an added line above the autograph thanking them for being awesome and helping out a good cause. This does two things: it helps the cause, and it gets my name out there.

You can try variations on this – perhaps pinning a card to the item, etc.

Or you can be a better person than I, and donate without any strings – and probably become my Mom's new favorite individual. The important thing is that you give back to your community when you can. You never know when *you* might be the one in need.

T-Shirts: The Mobile Billboards You Need

Let's talk about mobile billboards. All right, you might call them by their other name: t-shirts.

Everyone in this world (well, most people), from Bill Gates to Crazy Dave who sleeps under the bridge, enjoys free things. If you have family and friends, they probably fall into this category as well. Giving away t-shirts is a great way to get your name and logo out there, without having to actually *be* 'out there'. Although, I'm already 'out there', but not in the same way and… never mind.

At any rate, make sure you have the appropriate size for the individual on the receiving end, so that they don't end up on www.PeopleofWalMart.com.

Likewise, attach a 'string' to the gift:

> "Hey, Uncle Pete, please wear this to >where your target business would go<, and not the poodle strip club. Thanks!"

If you plan, and manipulate the gift a bit, it can be a great way to develop brand recognition, at less than ten bucks a pop. Plus, no one has to see Weird Uncle Pete's hairy back and moobies, so you're actually doing a public service as well.

If You Can't, *VistaPrint* Often Can

Being in business can be expensive.

No, scratch that, it *is* expensive.

So why splurge on lobster, when fish can be just as good*?

*(Besides – it all ends up the same).

The good folks at *VistaPrint* have taken the time to focus on you – the cottage, small, or medium sized business, as their target client market. And they've done an amazing job with it, to the tune of nearly 10 million customers.

What they offer is a virtual marketing store for a number of your key business needs. And they offer it at a more than reasonable cost, in an intuitive way that anyone from a novice to a ninja can divine and comprehend. Plus, you can shop right from the convenience of your own computer.

Never heard of them?

Then fire up your search engine of choice, do a search, and then pop on over to their site. You won't believe the variety and depth of the things they offer.

Make The Most Of Your Business Cards

Business cards have a backside – just like all of us (unless you're in a sideshow, or you're Kim Jong Un - then I'm sorry for having offended you).

Why do so many individuals leave them blank, though?

Perhaps they don't know what in the world to put back there.

I have a suggestion, because I'm self-promotional, and like to see the results of myself typing.

On the back of our *Digital Ninjas Media, Inc.* cards, we have individual, robust, QR codes, and our mission statement. It's a great way to show our clients something more than just a name and a pretty picture and – in the age of smart phones – it allows them to take our data and integrate it into their lives at the touch of a screen.

So the next time that you decide to purchase business cards, think long and hard about filling that extra space in the rear!*

*(I know, I know but – please – no jokes. I've already stopped myself twice. And if I can't make them, then you have to restrain yourself as well.)

Make Even More Use Of Your Business Cards

Speaking of Business Cards, my wife, Wanda, and I are geeking back-to-back in the fortress of geekdom (i.e. – our tech-ed-out office), and she just now said something simple, but brilliant.

She's been placing our business cards in the 'win a free lunch' containers at local restaurants. *But*, she's been making sure that our card is facing outward, against the glass, and is upright and bolstered by the others in the container, thereby making it the only one readable. And the shocking blue color makes it an instant eye catcher.

Way to think outside the box – er, container – dear!

Extra! Extra! Read All About It - But Only If You Make It Happen

Press releases: everyone's heard of them, but how many of you know what they *really* are, or how to make one?

Hands?

Anyone?

Weird Uncle Pete, you only need to put one hand up, thanks.

Okay, so some of you know – and some of you don't. And that's okay! If you're in the second camp, then here are some pointers for you to consider when crafting your own:

- The press release is like a partial résumé for your business. It outlines an experience or information about who you are, and what you're up to.
- Make it interesting! No one cares if you sold two widgets this month. What they care about is WHY that's compelling. Tell a story, and draw your audience in.
- Issue a press release quarterly. That's right, I said quarterly. Make it fresh, interesting, and relevant. Not everyone will print it. In point of fact, no one may. But that's okay! You're only out a stamp (or, in more recent times, an e-mail), and you've gained further experience toward writing the next one.
- Make sure you format it correctly, and get it into the

right hands! Botching either could make your whole effort an exercise in futility.
- Words are incredibly powerful tools. So use them well, and use them wisely.

Often, when we at *Digital Ninjas Media, Inc.* work on résumés for individuals, we find that what they think is an amazing résumé is really a study in poor writing skills. It's not their fault. They do what they do, and presumably do it well. If they're not professional writers, then it's almost to be expected. We spend copious amounts of time crafting a perfect résumé. One that uses all the right words, has a fluid dynamic to it, and is succinct while still being informative and engaging. It's a skill, and it's a difficult one to master.

As a published author myself*, I learn something every time I sit down to write. I write several blogs, I work on my books, I work on the books of others through ghostwriting or rough editing, and I handle all of the correspondence for my day job as well.

So if you're genuinely interested in better writing, then practice, practice, practice!

Start a blog, if for no other reason than to muse on the day's happenings and hone your writing skill by considering how to make your otherwise boring day seem interesting. And who knows – as you gain skill and become more adept, you might even pick up readership, or find a niche to focus on when writing.

*(See how I keep working that in until you're sick of hearing it?)

Visual Guerrilla Marketing: Don't Miss Your Opportunity!

Are you planning a public advertisement?

Then why not make it an *interactive* one?

Here's what I mean:

Say you're doing a billboard, or a window poster, or whatever. Create an area within the ad where an individual can stand, or sit, to be photographed. I've seen things like giant afro wigs, silly costumes, etc.

An ad like this does two things: it acts as an ad normally would*, but it also gets individuals to consider it more closely, and for a longer period of time. When they interact with it, hopefully they'll take a picture to show their friends, post it (or make reference to it) on a social site, on a blog, or just to 'make Mom proud' (can you hear the facetiousness in that last one?) And in that picture, why, there are your LOGO and SLOGAN!

*(Duh, Heath!)

So the next time you're spending hard-earned advertising money, make it go even farther – with a visually interactive ad!

Contests: A New Spin On Attraction Marketing

Sometimes, the only marketing tools you need are a brain and a physical store.

Have both?

Then this one is for you!

Let's say that you desire more business.

Because – well – who doesn't?

So come up with something that will sell itself, that you can host in your store location, even if it has nothing whatsoever to do with your store. Here's an example:

Let's say that you have a beauty supply company (I'm making this up as I go, so don't expect phenomenal creativity *all* of the time).

How about hosting a dog fashion show?

A 'cutest baby' contest?

A frog puppet competition?

You get the idea.

If it's a compelling enough concept, word of it will spread like wildfire. Putting some phone pole flyers, social media, web site and storefront hype, and web content to work for you wouldn't hurt either.

You could offer prizes of either free product, gift certificates to local establishments, or the king of all prizes – cold, hard, cash. Heck, Weird Uncle Pete could even emcee. Especially if there's poodles involved because, well, he has that certain, shall we say, 'unique penchant' for them that we've mentioned before.

So be creative, and make it happen!

Seminars & Workshops:
Make Your Potential Customers & Clients Come To You

If you're like me, you like to learn things. To be honest, I'm sort of a vacuum for knowledge. I crave it. I need it. It's something I live for. Okay, so I'm weird.

You don't have to live with me, so stop your complaining.

Let's pose a hypothetical question.

What if you're *really* good at what you do?

And what if what it is that you do isn't always the most easy to understand thing in the world?

Now you've got an opportunity.

What if you took that knowledge, and offered a no-cost, or low-cost, seminar or workshop on a topic that is relevant to your potential customers, but not often understood by them?

For the time and effort it takes, you might gain a new customer. And if they enjoy working with you (or eating what you make, or whatever – I can't cover everything), they're apt to make mention of that fact to their friends and family at large.

The Apprentice: Helping Your Community While Helping Yourself

Want to better your community at large, and make a difference in someone's life?

If you answered in the affirmative, then maybe it's time for you to have an apprenticeship program or apprentice program competition.

First, inform the local media that your business will be playing host to an apprenticeship, or an apprentice program competition of some sort to find a suitable apprenticeship candidate. You could find a youth who might not otherwise be exposed to this sort of business, a veteran who is having a tough time re-adjusting, or a homeless individual who just needs a leg up, allowing them to learn from your experience and to grow on a personal level.

While it's more work than typical marketing might be, it also gives something back to the community at large. It can also make a lasting impact on the life of another human being.

And who doesn't want a piece of that action?

Your License To Be Creative

As I'm driving around town, I find that I'm gaining knowledge from other drivers around me without even really thinking about it. I know the tan SUV in front of me may very well contain Megan's Mom. I know that the dude next to me in the destroyed '82 Camaro is totally into Zeppelin. And I know that the guy I passed two cars back is most likely a real estate salesperson.

How do I know all of these things?

It's simple: their license plates told me so.

What do your license plates tell people?

What?

Nothing, you say?

Well, why not?

If your vehicle – personal or business – is out and about a lot, it might be worth adding this one little touch to the front and back of your ride of choice. They're conversation starters, they can be funny, or they can just say what you do or sell.

If folks see them enough, they might even ask questions like, "Hey! What does that mean?" etc.

One thing you will want to avoid, however, is the clearly identifiable 'bad motorist syndrome'. My wife can tell me who drives like a douche-canoe on her way to work, any time we see them out and about.

Why?

It was all thanks to their vanity plates.

So make sure that you don't fall into *that* category. Because my wife and I still have plenty of vehicular distaste to go around.

All A-Board!

All A-board!

No, no, not ABOARD – *A-Board*!

A-boards can be a great way to increase visibility for your business in a perpendicular manner.

"Heath," I hear you saying, "What in the whoosafudge does that even *mean*?"

Here's the low-down:

If your storefront is located in a cityscape, then most likely you're visibility is limited to a straight-on view of your place of business. Perhaps, if you're lucky, you have a sign that hangs over the shop perpendicularly so as to gain more eyeballs in a 90º plane. But – typically – that's up high. You might not even be fortunate enough to have that much going for you.

Enter: the A-Board. These are simple creations that have two sides, with some sort of hinge mechanism at the top. You've seen them before. They're often outside of bistros and coffee houses, advertising the day's specials.

They work splendidly for *those* businesses – so why not yours?

I recommend developing either one, or a series, which can be changed or manipulated over time. Chalk board paint, floating letter channels, or a hook and plate system are all ways to make this happen, without having to go through a major overhaul to change the message, or causing you to have a ton of the things on hand for all occasions.

Further, you can make you're a-board stand out by taking the marketing premise from two-dimensional to three. Imagine one in the shape of a woman: you could put a skirt on her that blows up in the wind, revealing a message. Or you could cut a hole in the boards, put a pair of flap overalls on it (making it look like someone is farting when the wind blows). There are so many things you can do, if you just put your mind, and a little imagination into it.

Be A Guest Star - Even If You're Not Famous

Have you ever watched late night television and wondered how they get all of those famous folks on those shows to be interviewed?

Turns out, it's not just benevolence, narcissism, or boredom. Those guests are there for a reason. And more often than not, their publicist, manager, or distributing media empire got them there.

It's a classic study in symbiotic relations. Like bees and flowers, each has a need that only the other may best satisfy. Guests need to hawk something they're doing/selling, etc. and the hosts need interesting guests to make their show ratings-worthy.

"That's great," you might say, "But I'm not famous, you're not famous, and Weird Uncle Pete is the only one I know who is, but for all the wrong reasons. And I am >NOT< attaching my name to *that* man!

At least, not again."

Hey: I hear you!

What you may have, however, is a blog. If you do, then you can take a similar approach to symbiosis as the rich and (in)famous.

What if you found a blog of equal stature, where you could offer to swap a 'guest' spot with the owner of that blog?

You would provide a guest entry for their blog for a day and they, in turn, would do likewise for you. Suddenly, you're reaching a whole new audience who, if written well, may be very inclined to be interested in what you have to say down the line.

If not, then so what?

What are you out?

Less than an hour crafting a post, that's what. That seems like a small price to pay for the potential inherent in the transaction.

So get out there, and be a resounding guest star!

Testify, Sisters & Brothers In Business!

Customer testimonials: at one time, they were far more meaningful than they are now. At least, that's my opinion. With the advent of instantaneous feedback, their relevance has become somewhat more muted (again, my personal opinion). Yet that isn't to say that they don't have worth or usefulness in this day and age.

Every day in your business, you interact with clients. And every interaction is an opportunity for you, your product, or a coupling of the two to either wow them, force them into indifference, or royally cheese them off.

Okay, there are varying degrees in there, but you get the idea.

Further, your physical store or sales space may also be a factor in swaying a positive reaction – you just never know what folks will latch on to, so be prepared for anything.

Before I go any further, remember this: some feedback, no matter how awesome you are, will be negative.

Why?

Well, because you might not be on you're a-game, or more likely some folks are just jerks.

It's true.

For your purposes, it probably isn't a good idea to allow the 'Jerk' or 'Disaffected' folks to be quoted. What is important about them, however, is how you handle them, and what you do to try and bring them back into the other camp.

What we're looking for, in this instance, are the folks who develop a passion for your products. Folks who love your store, love you, or can't live without whatever you are selling. These are the folks you really want to focus on: the gushers of positive energy.

When you encounter one of these folks (and you'll know it, believe me, because on the rare occasions when I am one, I will go all stupid and misty eyed over something I'm impressed with to the point of seeming irrational and high), take a moment to ask if they'd like for their voice to be heard. Specifically, provide them with an opportunity to write a testimonial. And then, convince them how important it is you, and your business, so that they do not fail to follow through. Be prepared, though: even the most well-meaning individuals will forget you – and your store or product – in the short term. Not intentionally, but because life throws more pressing things at them.

The Holy Grail of testimonials is gaining the favor of individuals who have some semblance of following or fame. Imagine how great it would be if, say, Rick Bayliss showed up at your Mexican restaurant, said he liked your food, and you convinced him to pose for a photo with you, while writing down – verbatim – a testimonial direct from his mouth. Then, you hang the picture, with the quotation proudly beneath it, and your restaurant just gained a ton of street cred and mouth-to-mouth acclaim.

And all you had to do was be prepared.

In the end, every business is different. With this being so, it is still possible to make use of the testimonial – even if the means and method vary.

So start your collection today! You don't have to use them all, but the more you gather, the more you'll have to choose from (and potentially exhibit for the world at large to see, and consider).

Please Refer To... You!

Referrals: They've been around for ages. In fact, I can mentally picture Oog giving Ock a 20% larger club for his having referred his cousin, Smook, who purchased a club from him just last week.

To some degree, referrals are one of the highest compliments that your consumers and clients can pay you.

Why?

Think about it: would you stick your neck out for a business that didn't treat you well?

Would you want to be responsible for recommending that veterinarian who, somehow, accidentally spayed Aunt Mabel's cat, even though it was male?

Of course not!

Personally, I am more than reluctant to refer anyone to anyone else, or anywhere else. But – when I do – my acquaintances know me well enough to know that it's a lock. That referral is sound, and they'd be a sucker not to listen. I also have friends who, when a recommendation is made, I follow it unquestioningly because I know they're like me in this sense.

Encouraging referrals is always recommended. In fact, I would recommend putting the specifics right on your door, entrance side and exit side, so that the first and last thing that your clients see is that resounding message. Then, you can periodically take it a step further. To do so, you will have to remember two inalienable truths:

- People are inherently lazy
- You will need something profoundly worth it to them to negate truth #1

This is where freebies, coupons, and discounts come in. Think of something that you can give up, without breaking the bank, but that's also not so Chintzy as to make it a non-starter.

I've seen so many 'referral' campaigns fail.

Truth be told, some are just downright stupid.

I can save a dollar on a $25.00 purchase with a referral and two coupons?

Who in the world cares?

That sounds waaay too much like work to me. Give me something I can sink my financial teeth into.

One of the most egregious offenders, in my personal opinion, are the satellite television providers. They offer $50.00 for a referral. Not a bad chunk of change, but considering what it will take to get someone to switch carriers, not exactly a stellar incentive, either. Were it up to me, I'd up the stakes, and look at the big picture.

How about $250.00 for a referral?

Now you've got my attention – now I'm motivated. Heck, now I'm a veritable Apostle for your business venture. It will take you far longer to make up the lost revenue, but over time you're still set to make a profit that you might otherwise have missed altogether.

See the difference?

This is why it's so important to quantify the 'quality' of the referral incentive. Give as much up as you possibly can in the now, for the rewards in the immediate aftermath, and then down the road. Consider it well. Above all, make it simple. REALLY, REALLY, REALLY, SIMPLE – and then see what happens. If it doesn't work as you would have liked, ask for feedback.

Why aren't folks referring?

What would incite them to do so, that you're not already doing?

Be flexible until you get it honed to perfection, and then be amazed with the results.

Give It Away, And See If It Returns

Sometimes, giving your services away can be the most rewarding marketing that you can do.

I hear you, I hear you: "Uh, what now?

"Have you gone mental?

"Have you been hanging with Weird Uncle Pete again?!"

To which I say: You read that right; no; and oh *heck* no!

Here's what I mean:

Let's say you're the proprietress of a hair salon.

Why?

Because I need an example.

Wouldn't it be nice to be known as the hair salon that cares about their community?

But how would one make that work?

Well, what if you offered your services for free?

It sounds crazy, but hear me out.

What if, for one day, you offered a free haircut to food pantry patrons; to returning veterans; to shut-ins; to nursing home residents; to job seekers through a temporary agency?

How about if you stayed open for 24 hours to help out those who work weird hours get a haircut, once a month?

You could even let the authorities know ahead of time, if you're concerned about safety. Perhaps they would be willing to assist with extra patrols, or a nice off duty officer might be willing to trade a couple haircuts for keeping an eye on the place.

Suffice it to say, the possibilities are beyond myriad. The return comes in letting the press know ahead of time what you're doing. Submit a press release to everyone you can find, and follow up with phone calls. Those agencies and services are there to let people know about things happening in their local world. And if they're doing it right, they'll do just that.

What's the best-case scenario?

You get a snippet on the news and a warm feeling.

And who doesn't want *that* for free?

This idea can be applied to numerous businesses. In fact, we have a client (an Auto Repair Shop) who cyclically offers oil changes in exchange for donations to local causes that they believe in. And that balanced benevolence has gained them a phenomenal following when those same folks need their vehicles serviced.

Give it some serious thought. Get feedback from friends, family, and customers. If it looks like something that will work – do it!

Your community is important, and you can make a difference.

Start A Group - And Then Allow Them To Reward You For Doing So

Have you ever considered personal growth, while inadvertently marketing and teaching?

Okay – probably not.

But what if you could do all of those wonderful things in one go?

Well, you can!

Why not start a special interest group?

You could allow individuals to sign up, use your store space, and meet (perhaps, a couple of times a month) to discuss your common ground, have workshops, or monthly projects. The possibilities are voluminous because – well – your businesses are all different. You could even charge a nominal fee for the club, make t-shirts, and on and on.

The goal?

To soft-sell product, increase your customer base, and generate customer loyalty by communing with them regularly. Or at the very least, allowing them a place in which to commune amongst themselves.

Who Are Your Customers? The Fish Know!

The business card fishbowl: you've all seen them. They're those glass containers found in stores or restaurants, into which you toss one of your business cards in the hopes of winning something that is free (whether you actually need it or not).

You do have one in your business establishment, don't you?

Wait, what?

You *don't*?!

Well that won't do at all!

For those of you that do, kudos! You're dismissed from this segment.

Now for the rest of you, I offer the remainder of this segment.

These business card accumulation vessels are there for a reason. They provide hundreds of leads while quantifying who your clients actually are.

Do you serve a lot of lawyers?

Doctors?

Hippo trainers?

These cards can tell you a lot, if you're willing to take the time to listen and pay attention. They can also provide leads for cross-pollination marketing. Most will also contain an e-mail address. You could exploit this facet by adding a disclaimer in the body of the contest rules posted, advising them that by participating they are opting-in to e-mail receipt. In this way, those that choose not to do so have fair warning. But when you *do* send e-mail, make it something special or worthwhile. Or you'll lose them just as quickly as you gained them.

There's a ton of things that you can do with the cards, although each idea will be specific and different for each business-type out there. So give it a go, learn who your customers are, and give them something they hope to win. It's a cheap way to hone in on who your customer base really is. And that data can be exceptionally valuable.

Hear Ye, Hear Ye: I Have A Business, And I'm Keen!

The Salvation Army bell ringer: you've all seen them before. Hopefully, you've chosen to put a few doubloons into their ubiquitous red pails as well. If not, then I'm totally sticking my tongue out at you right now. These intrepid souls brave the cold, irritating repetition of high-pitched dinging, and, sometimes, outright scorn.

And for what?

Because they want to help individuals that they will never meet, who are less fortunate then they themselves are. It doesn't get much more benevolent than that. It can be a humbling experience, as well as an exercise in personal appreciation of one's own life. Trust me: if you're reading this, then you don't have it that bad.

So now we come to you.

Have you ever done this?

I personally have not. My wife and I support a local food pantry monetarily – and she with volunteering two Monday evenings a month as well, because she's a heck of a lot nicer than I am. She also helps the homeless and less fortunate with preparing for job interviews, résumés and work attire, because she didn't feel like she was doing enough.

Can you tell that I'm proud of her?

All right, I digress. But she really is amazing.

Now for those of you who play no active role in giving to causes, or cannot due to financial constraints, then what better way to do something than to volunteer your time as a bell ringer?

Your time has value, and it won't put a strain on your pocketbook. It's still giving, and it still totally counts.

"That's great, Heath. But what in the whoosafudge does this have to do with marketing?"

I'm getting there, I promise.

Ready?

What if you were to wear your corporate shirt/jacket/hat/mittens/button/other while doing so?

Here is an opportunity to be seen as a righteous dude (or dude-ette, depending on the plumbing God gave you), and also to get thousands of new eyeballs on your company logo. You're helping out a good cause, you're getting your business noticed, and you may even feel all warm and fuzzy inside. And while that could be from that Irished-up coffee you drank beforehand, I'll just pretend that it's really because doing nice things makes you feel that way.

So go forth, ring the annoying little bell, collect some cash-ola for the less fortunate, and get your business noticed while you're at it.

It's a win-win!

Your Own Personal Christmas Wonderland-Nirvana

First, let me start by saying that if you're a Jehovah's Witness, of the Jewish Faith, an Atheist, Muslim, Buddhist, Taoist, of any other denomination, faith, or creed not mentioned, or a devout Christian who is upset that we've forgotten what Christmas is supposed to be about, that I mean no disrespect by the following section. It's meant purely as a marketing idea based on the societal circumstances occurring, or about to occur, around us (depending on when you're reading this), and nothing more.

And now, the idea: the Christmas Scene.

It seems that over the years, the Chinese industrial complex has become extremely adept at figuring out ways for we here in America to have bigger, better, more interesting, and complex things to put on our house and lawn during the holiday seasons. And we've accepted it like one might a dying, rich Uncle who also smells nice and secretly tells you that you've always been his favorite.

It used to be just a single-bulb, burning inside of an injection-molded Santa with a little wooden sign. Now we can create a cacophony of sights and sounds in our own front yard that would rival *Disneyland* in the 50's or a Discotheque in the 70's.

For me, it's all a bit much. But if you've got the seasonal hardware (or have been looking for an excuse to let that festive elf out of you, to run wild) then it might be a great way to 'tie-in' your business.

How?

The easiest way is to develop a theme which is business-centered, but still allows for the Christmas theme to be present. Focus the activity, scene, or items in a way that draws attention to the business at the core of the display. Better still: if at all possible, have the display characters or scene actually depicting your business activity.

Who wouldn't want to see elves doing accounting, and Santa using *QuickBooks*?

Heck, even *I* want to see that.

Be strategic, plan ahead, have your non-weird Uncle Fred paint up some plywood to fill in the blanks, and go nuts.

One word of warning, though: If I see baby Jesus, Mary, Joseph, Gaspar, Melchior, or Balthazar personally hawking anything in your display, you will receive a stern rap across the knuckles with a ruler. I might even go and find a nun who remembers me fondly from High School for an assist. So don't do it.

Participating In Local Festivals: Your Ticket To Static Advertising Notoriety

A number of major and minor metropolitan areas have Christmas-specific events. For instance, in the city where I grew up, we had a major international snow sculpting competition. Tied in with that, we also had a parallel event called, *'The Festival of Lights'*. It afforded local businesses, individuals, and institutions the opportunity to create a scene or piece of lighted art of any sort (within the guidelines) to be viewed in a forested park at night. The host city set it up so that one would drive through the entire park on its single, meandering roadway. Along the way, these scenes greeted you, and yourself (and your kids, more so), enjoyed the experience.

I don't specifically recall what the numbers are for visitors to the display, but suffice it to say it's astronomical. Further, it draws individuals from not only the host city, but also from surrounding areas and towns, as well as professional snow sculpting teams from around the world.

This is where you come in.

If you have something like this in your area, you could register to create a scene or sculpture of your own. I would recommend something that shows what your business does, is visually informative, and espouses your values. I realize that sounds great in concept. Creating it in practice does take some thought and craftsmanship though, I'll grant you.

Give it a try!

It will take a few bucks, some time, and creativity. But you could opt to include employees in the production of the scene. Friends and family are usually looking for an excuse to hang out, so use this as an excuse to create one!

Whatever you do, keep it tasteful, keep in mind who you want to reach and – most of all – make it visually compelling.

Be A Cog In The Machine For Social Good

In my locale, we have several recurring, annual, charity drives. Most come up around the holidays, and most center around toys for local, underprivileged children. Others involve veterans, the elderly, and probably more stuff I would know about if I paid more attention in my day-to-day life, or read those pamphlets Weird Uncle Pete keeps sending me.

The bottom line: someone's doing something about something, and making a difference. So they're all good.

To the point: a number of these outreach programs are widespread, in order to have the highest impact. To do this, these organizations/programs enlist the assistance of local businesses as designated 'drop sites'. And this is where your business comes in.

Now if you don't have a physical workspace, then this probably isn't for you. You get the day off from this entry, if you like.

For the rest of you, I would encourage you to find a cause that parallels your views and beliefs. Then contact the primary sponsor or organizer of said program to inquire as to how your business might become a drop site.

This does two things.

First, it makes you feel good because you're helping to enlarge the scope of the giving.

Second, it gives your business positive exposure to potential customers/clients that might not otherwise know you exist. And a strong first impression is everything. They're already there to participate in your benevolence – great! Now make sure that you treat them like your #1 customer, because someday they might be. Greet them, chat with them if they seem open to the idea. Most of all, be Über-friendly.

Can't find a program that you like?

You could develop your own – there's nothing wrong with that. But remember that if you do, *YOU* will be responsible for development, implementation, and promotion. If you've got the time, money, and energy – go for it. But for the rest of us, I would encourage participation alone. It's still for social and community good, and it's still totally worthwhile.

I Don't Love A Parade, But Your Customers May

Oh, how I love a parade!

Okay, that's a complete lie. I actually hate the things. Let me be more succinct, here: I like watching the multi-million dollar ones on television during the holidays when I can eat leftovers in my pajamas. I don't like the local ones, because I'm lazy, I'm high-maintenance in the entertainment department, and cold and I haven't spoken since I was eleven.

But that's okay!

Who the heck needs my grumpy ass curmudging their event, anyway?

Wait, is that even a word?

This is about you!

Many parades are sponsored by local Chambers of Commerce, while others are sponsored by local Governmental or Social entities. And all of them are an opportunity to gain recognition for your business from a great many folks, all in one go.

So what can you do about it?

Here's my recommendation: participate.

Here's my second recommendation: if you do, go big or go home. In the few parades I have participated in (don't ask) it was clear who the eyeball winners and losers were. If you're carrying a plain white banner that says, '*Local Oven Mitt Collectors Club*', then you're already in trouble - especially if the float or attraction in front of, or behind you, are more interesting. And unless they're a social club of stoic undertakers standing still, they will be.

When I was sixteen, I worked for a short while at a comic book emporium in an adjoining city (remember that from a number of pages back?) When the time for the local parade came around, the owner had an idea: he would contact *Marvel* and contract *Spider-Man* out for the day. And that one spandex clad dude (his real name was Jacques, and he was super nice, if you want to know his secret identity) *STOLE-THE-SHOW*. Every eyeball for sixty feet either way was on him, as he capered about, high-fived kids, and had his picture taken more times than a drunken celebrity. We (the comic book store lackeys) followed behind, and handed out flyers for the '*Spider Man After-Party*' to be held at the comic book store.

When the parade was over, we returned to the store. A now jam-packed, probably fire code-violating, store. Kids and parents stood in line for pictures, smiles were everywhere, and we sold a gazillion dollars of merchandise – a goodly amount of it, not surprisingly – *Spider-Man* related.

I can't even factor the return on investment this single idea brought, nor the potential new customers who had never been to the store.

I also can't quantify how many times that day I heard, "I knew you were here, but I never stopped in." Or, "I didn't know you sold >*Item In Question Here*<!"

So this is why I say go big, or go home: because I can't tell you who was in front of, or behind us, in that parade. And I'll bet no one else could, either.

Game On!

Looking for a unique way to reach potential clients all sports-season long?

Why not sponsor a sports team?

With the advent of budget cuts at many public schools, more and more children (and their parents) are seeking alternative outlets for all of that pent-up energy. And since Scotch isn't recommended for minors, they tend to lean more towards sports. And these sports need sponsors. And those players need jerseys: *your* jerseys, with *your* business information on them.

So the kids get to play and avoid potential alcoholism, the adults get to rest when the kids are worn out, and every single eyeball at every game – all season – will see your company's information front and (possibly) center. And each week, a new team is typically played. This fact brings with it a whole new set of eyeballs.

If you don't own a kid-friendly business (i.e. – a strip club, or a bar, let's say) then how about adult teams?

And no, I don't mean that kind you weirdoes. I mean pool leagues, dart leagues and – my personal favorite – bowling leagues!

If it's a good fit for your business model, then do something that benefits kids growing up right, or adults blowing off steam, and also gets your business exposure that you might not otherwise have received.

Gift Baskets: The Love And Hate Of Them

This delightful monologue centers on a phenomena that I personally don't have an affinity for. But for some reason, it's a phenomena that inexplicably allows both purchasers and receivers to be momentarily blinded by the actual (lack of) value of the product that they're giving or receiving: The Gift Basket.

These things are a work of genius.

Why?

Because the effort of constructing them is typically (more on the 'typically' bit further on) not proportional to the value then placed upon them. And this is the key idea behind this segment.

Let's begin with me, because I'm narcissistic that way. A few years back, for Christmas, I received a very thoughtful mini gift basket from a co-worker. It was *Simpsons*-themed (and it showed he was paying attention to what I liked), and appeared to be chock full of fun stuff. When I opened it, instead of just appreciating the gift (which I truly did, let it be known) I began to analyze the contents. Specifically, because there was a price tag still on the bottom that this individual had missed and subsequently not removed. As I deconstructed the thing, I realized that what it contained could be purchased at any local grocery store for about three dollars. The disconnect began and ended with the 'added value' of brand content (*The Simpsons*) and presentation (lots of colorful cellophane, paper, ribbons, and other stuff.) It really was a wondrous little package.

I didn't think too much more about it until about a year later when *Amazon.com* began running their annual '*Black Friday*' deals. Over the course of the days that unfolded, numerous gift baskets came up at special, 'discounted' pricing. Out of curiosity, I checked many of them out. And – to a one – they all contained a small amount of product in proportion to the price, 'discounted' or not. The difference in many of these was that they brought together an odd assortment of things otherwise difficult to put together (the decade-centric, retro candy boxes, for example) or had a gorgeous presentation that would ultimately be discarded moments after opening (the wine & cheese baskets, and the bath & body baskets). The craziest thing of all, to the pragmatist in me, was that folks can't seem to get enough of them. And this intrigued me further.

On the converse side of things, I have also seen a different sort of gift basket tactic. This one I will call the 'huge monetary value, low presentation value' type. These typically bundle a number of items that the vendor needs to get rid of. It's either inventory overstock, discontinued product, or a brand they are no longer going to carry. They put these baskets together to 'bundle in' slow movers. Then, they figure the MAXIMUM retail value of all the items, and tout that number, while putting a far lower, 'special' price on the whole affair.

And – voila - instant bargain!

But is it really?

Maybe if I had more hair to use hair products on, or used make up,* then sure.

*(These are just two examples that come to mind when I consider this method of marketing).

The point for you – as the seller – isn't always to create a reality. Rather, it is to create a *perceived* reality that your customers will (ideally) espouse.

For example: In the movie '*Sneakers*' (a geek favorite, by the way) there is a conversation being had by Ben Kingsley and Robert Redford's characters. They are hanging out near a *Cray* Supercomputer (awesome), and discussing perception versus reality. One mentions that if the false perception of banks failing can be perpetrated successfully on the public at large, their response will be to pull all of their money out of said banks –

thereby making the once perceived reality a hard reality, in fact. And it's a genius hypothesis. I realize that this might all sound harsh and callous. I guess it sort of is. But it's also marketing, at its core.

Here's what I offer, in conclusion: gift baskets work. The key seems to be to bundle intuitively or to make them glitter with the awe-inspiring beauty of a frosty winter morning, or a *Miss America Pageant* contestant. People seem drawn to give something that does, in fact, look gorgeous and that they don't have to wrap. This fact has value to them. The problem that you face is figuring out how to create a combination that has the maximum profit margins with the minimum amount of work.

I'm not saying be lazy. I'm suggesting that you be strategic.

This sort of marketing tactic is not only limited to holidays, or gift giving, as we have seen discussed above. It can also play on a customer's sense of value while you are afforded a way to blow out slow-moving or stagnant stock. This type is a win-win, if you can find a way to balance the value of the contents to the potential purchaser, while also affording yourself some marginal profit on items that just won't move.

Don't think it's for you?

Perhaps it's not. But I would encourage every one of you who reads this and has a product(s) line(s), to try it. After Christmas, hit the clearance sales. Look for things that sparkle, are unique, or will facilitate a good presentation for this experiment. Then find stock that has been around since the Reagan administration, or that your over-zealous employees inexplicably decided to buy three cases of. Merge them together in a pleasing manner. I can *almost* guarantee that you'll be amazed with the results.

Release your creative beast!

Rewards Programs: Your Psychological Friend

The rewards program is something that's been around for a very long time, in a number of guises. And it's something that I typically don't care for. Only – it turns out – I've been happily using one for almost two decades without even considering it. This made me take a step back, and re-assess their popularity to the general public as a collective. In doing so I realized that - as the whole - they're fairly effective marketing tools.

In my case, I'm an avid bibliophile. And for those of you who just cursed me for wanting to have sex with ducks, let me enlighten you, and expand your lexicon. Bibliophilia is, in fact, an intense love for books.

And no, I don't mean... meh, never mind.

I am a particular collector of rare, often signed, first edition books. These aren't your typical grocery store, newsstand types. Unfortunately they also don't cost the same as those types, either.

Years ago, I decided that I needed a second credit card. I wanted one that wasn't tied to my bank. After some searching, and not finding anything of particular interest, I happened upon one that allowed me to buy things and earn 'points' that would allow me to further my disease – er – hobby.

Guess which card I immediately picked?

So I now find myself guilty of utilizing something that I, in fact, purport not to care for: rewards programs.

Why don't I like them?

Because so many that I am familiar with don't so much seem to be rewards programs, as they are a leveling of the playing field between the vendor and the customer. The worst offenders here, in my personal opinion, are the grocery store and drug store programs. They seem to offer insanely high pricing, but give you a 'discount', 'rebate', or 'bonus' if you use their card. In my mind, prices being too high are never going to be any less than that. And asking me to use a card to bring them more into the realm of sanity seems, to me, kind of dumb.

I realize I'm in a minority here. I'm just trying to be honest. And – just possibly – I'm all backward on the whole thing. If I am, feel free to gently correct me. As long as it's constructive and enlightening, I can take it.

Anyway, back to the matter at hand: rewards programs. As discussed in previous sections (referring specifically to the 'referral incentive programs'), if you're going to do this, go big or go home. Give as much incentive as you possibly can without damaging your bottom line. Always, however, be considering the fact that repeat customers have an inherent value as well. Make certain to factor that into the equation. Find a program that truly rewards loyalty on the part of your customers, without being insensitive to the fact that they have the ability to think for themselves and can, in most cases, see through a poorly executed ruse.

Whether it's a punch card, quantity buying bonuses, store visit points, purchasing points, dollar value points – whatever – make certain that it's easy to understand, easy to follow, and rewards them in a way that you would wish to be rewarded. Get inside of their heads. Consider things from their point of view. Ask their opinions. Get their advice. And – most of all – plan for success. When done correctly, success will follow. And should it ever seem to falter, don't sit comfortably on your dwindling laurels. Find out where the disconnect is occurring, and make every effort to rectify it as soon as is humanly possible. Otherwise, all of your hard work – and the program itself – means nothing.

Clone Your Ad & Stare Your Potential
Customers In The Face While They Shop

Here's an idea that many service providers and service-oriented vendors have already latched on to, but that might have blown right past you: the shopping cart advertisement.

These things are *brilliant*. These ads afford their advertising entities a widely varying, captive audience. And better still, the ads can be tailored to advertise within a highly specific region via this method.

If you don't know what I'm talking about, then I'll assume you just returned from an important, top-secret, Government space pilgrimage that lasted about thirty years or so.

So first: welcome back to Earth! There have been a number of changes while you were gone, including this method of advertising.

What I'm talking about are those little signs that are 'embedded' into special frameworks either in the seats, seat flaps, front, sides, or bottoms of shopping carts. While you're looking in your purse at your shopping list, or pondering what compelled you to pick up thirteen cans of oyster stew, there they are, staring back at you, advertising the whole time you're there.

They work even harder by advertising to the employees of the store, day in and day out. Every day, those hard-working folks are inadvertently viewing those ads as they work their shifts. And every one of those glances is a potential opportunity for a new client or a sale.

I don't necessarily recommend these signs for low-volume, non-repeat sales. They seem to be best for service providers who attain perpetual clients: accountants, attorneys, insurance agents, real estate – these are all home-run businesses for this type of advertising.

Do yourself a favor, and see what it's all about. You might find that it offers an amazing return on investment.

Stick To The Small Stuff

I don't know about you but – for me – sticky notes are something that I can no longer live without. I use them in two different sizes, and for all sorts of different things in my daily work life. To say that they're indispensable is probably a foregone conclusion. And were I to ever run into Art Fry in a bar, all his drinks for the evening would be on me (even if his invention was somewhat accidental in nature).

A few of my larger vendors bring me 'premiums' from time to time. Often, I give them away to co-workers because I don't use them personally. Sticky notes – on the other hand – I usually hang on to. Poster sized wall calendars and oversized mouse pads are the other items that I have been known to hang on to. The rest I could take or leave*, in case you were curious.

*(Unless it's a t-shirt [but, seriously, it has to *fit* - I am not a *Keebler* elf, vendors]. That, at least, should be obvious as my 6' 3" frame towers over you every time we talk. To date, I have never received a t-shirt that even comes close to fitting anything larger than my cat.)

All right, I digress - back to the matter at hand. These sticky notes that these vendors so graciously provide have been emblazoned with their company logo, company name, slogan, or a combination of the three.

They've been professionally printed, and I can assume are not free to have made. What these sticky notes do, in my specific case, is remind me every time I look at my desk, or reach for one, who gave them to me. Their brand is getting eyeball time. Lots of eyeball time.

The problem for these vendors in particular, unfortunately, is that I've been using their product for years and never really forget who they are. Still, there's a value to them, nonetheless. Because when I use one in front of a customer, another vendor, or other individual, *that person* now sees the branding, too. And quite often, these are the same folks who come to me to 'pick my brain' (I hate that term, by the way) about sourcing things.

In the end, it's inadvertent exposure for the vendor that was never intended, but has just pushed the visibility of the brand that much further.

One of my vendor's salespersons has put his own spin on this idea. What this fellow has done is to have a custom rubber stamp made up that says something like, "Stick with Me for your needs". What's unique about this tactic is that it costs him far less than having the sticky notes professionally prepared. He's taking the idea of branding even further down the supply chain by branding not only his business as a solution provider but *himself* as one as well.

Regardless of how you consider this idea for your own business, consider taking that extra step and branding yourself as a solution provider in tandem with the business. And definitely consider this gentleman's inexpensive solution to a potentially huge printing bill.

Come On In!

Want to stir up more business?

Want to make your neighborhood aware of your existence, and what it is that you and your business do?

Want free advertising to do all of these things?

Then – congratulations – get ready to have an open house!

Open houses are a great tool that businesses employ for all of the above reasons, as well as numerous others. It gives you the opportunity to get folks in the door who might not otherwise know you were there. It helps you connect with the neighbors around your business, and it allows the new folks to meet you on a more human level. It can also provide an opportunity for folks you've talked to on the phone over the years to come and meet you in person.

To make an open house a success, a number of things should be considered:

Thing 1: Offer refreshments. Offering free grub and beverages is a sure way to get folks to stop in because, let's face it, we all like something for nothing, even if it's a hot dog, and we have to drive fifteen minutes to get it.

Crazy, huh?

Thing 2: Hold a raffle or give door prizes. Advise clearly, in all the distributed media, what the grand prize(s) will be, what the rules are, and how one manages to participate. Referring back to Thing 1: we all like something for nothing.

Thing 3: Let your local paper(s) and television news outlet(s) know what's happening. Often, they'll run it in the Events Calendar of the paper at no charge. If it's a slow news day, they might even drop by and run news of your event as a 'filler' or 'public/human interest' story.

Thing 4: Let other avenues know what's up as well. Talk to your neighboring businesses about putting up posters in their shops.

Why would they want to?

Because you're about to increase traffic to your place of business, and they're in close proximity. In essence, you're benefiting them by association. Hand out leaflets to your existing customers (slip it in their bag when they check out), post it on your social media and web sites, and – if the law in your area allows – *responsibly* blanket the neighborhood with leaflets. And when the event is over, make sure to take them down and recycle them. You don't need to be adding to the mess this planet now finds itself in. No one likes *that* person, so don't *be* that person.

Thing 5: Offer specials. Have special deals, sales, etc. in place for that day, thereby sweetening the pot even further. Folks inherently like to feel like they're getting a good deal on stuff.

Thing 6: Consider offering premiums on your big day. Give away branded or logoed *Frisbees*, mugs – whatever. People like something for nothing.

Have I mentioned that yet?

Thing 7: Prepare to handle the deluge. I would recommend that you ask all staff to be on hand that day, if for no other reason than to act as docents. This way the flow of business is not staunched, and the attendees may also take the time to talk to you, or one of your associates, about your business, the weather, their dog Fluffy – whatever. The point is to be accessible to these good folks who came here because they love something for nothing. They're here – now network, and market to them!

Some other thoughts to be advised of:

- Make sure that you don't need a permit to do something like this.
- Make sure that there is adequate parking available.
- Make sure that you know what your structure's maximum occupancy is. You don't want the Fire Marshall on your butt.
- Make sure the structural integrity of the building you're hosting The event in can handle a mass of people. I know that this probably sounds stupid but – trust me – it isn't.
- Shoplifters work well in crowds
- And above all else, have fun! This is a rare chance to be the center of attention. It was a lot of work getting there, so enjoy the moment!

Is It Cold In Here? No. That's Just You

The cold call: it's something that few have the patience, skill, charisma, or persistence for. I include myself in that statement, because I'm lousy at them. Plus, I just hate the things in general. In fact, I would rather do my own dental work than go on a cold call.

Sometimes, for the sake of our respective businesses, however, it's a necessary evil. So assuming that it's either a necessary evil for you, something you want to explore trying, or you're a sadist, then here are some helpful hints to (potentially) make it more successful:

Hint #1: Who are you calling on?

Before you even set foot out your door, you had better have your homework done.

You wouldn't go to work, and *then* get dressed, would you?

Cold calling functions in the same manner. All of your preparation needs to be done before you leave. And this means several things.

First and foremost, who (or what) business type are you targeting?

If you're just going door to door willy-nilly, then plan on wasting a ton of your time, and making others frustrated at your having wasted theirs.

Secondly, have you attempted to learn who it is within the potential customer's organization that you should be seeing?

Knowing this one small piece of information can drop a wary receptionist's defenses to a lower DefCon level. And every little bit helps.

Hint #2: Dress for success. Treat these cold calls as first dates. Dress confidently, smartly, and in a functionally matching wardrobe. I've seen guys come in looking like they've never worn the suit they're wearing before. Conversely, I've had others who came in where their wardrobe immediately said, "Listen to this guy – he's got it together!" If you don't have that 'killer app' suit or outfit, then find one. It's really, really important.

Hint #3: I don't want to know that you're a smoker, or be aware of what you had for lunch. It sounds obvious, but you'd be amazed how many cold calls I take where the folks smell like chimneys, garlic, beer, whiskey, or Italian dressing. And there's no faster way to shut me down and make me look for an exit than being malodorous. Likewise, if it's a hot day, plan to sweat. Wear plenty of deodorant, a moderate amount of cologne, etc. It might be that you have to stop home once or twice on a really hot day to shower. But I promise it will be the best-valued shower that you've ever taken.

In summation: mints are your friends. Borrow a non-smoker's vehicle, or use one that is not smoked in. Freshly launder your clothing and then immediately remove it from a smoky environment if you're an indoor smoker. Trust me on this.

Hint #4: Remember that time is money. If someone deigns to see you unannounced, then count your blessings.

Now – don't blow it!

Have your spiel down pat – short and sweet. Consider having a packet of further detailed information to leave for later perusal on the potential client's part. Listen more than you talk when possible. And be prepared to defend yourself when a question is asked!

Hint #5: Don't go during 'bad' times of the day. If you come in between 11:30 and 1:30, expect the party to be at lunch. If you come in first thing in the morning, expect an immediate brush off from the receptionist. And if you come in at the end of the day, expect the same. Timing is critical – so make sure your timetables are set in a manner that allow for success.

Hint #6: Remember 'The Bubble'. I'm a guy who doesn't like to be touched. And nothing gets my hackles up faster than a space invader. I hate, hate, HATE space invaders. If you can't keep a respectable distance between us, then I'm not going to listen to you. I'm going to run... away... quickly.

Oh, and Weird Uncle Pete?

This goes for you as well.

Hint #7: Don't get discouraged!

I know: easier said than done. And I feel like a hypocrite for saying it because – well – I *do* get discouraged. But you can't let 'The Man' get you down. Keep plugging away. More importantly, review the situation that just occurred. Look for things that you could have done better or differently. Consider whether the potential client showed any 'tells', and consider when these 'tells' came to the fore. Arm yourself with that knowledge for the next call.

Hint #8: Just because they won't see you, doesn't mean you have to walk away without having accomplished something. If the receptionist says you would need to talk to Rick in Maintenance, then make a note of this for another time. Now you know their name. You're a step ahead from whence you began.

Also, consider leaving a packet of information for the potential client.

I would even suggest that you consider taking it a step further. Leave a short, concise, form letter with each packet stating why you feel they need your services. Otherwise, expect your packet-o-stuff to be round filed without a second glance. Unless you're insanely fortunate, they're not going to read it all to understand who you are.

Hint #9: Exude confidence. If you seem confident, then the other person will, typically, be subconsciously receptive to that. Smile, speak slowly and clearly. Emote friendliness, don't swear (you'd be amazed how many times a cold-caller swears when talking to me) and for the love of Peter, don't jabber on about personal stuff about yourself, unless it's relevant. Remember the old adage: me, me, me, is dull, dull, dull. Prepare to be excited about whatever *they're* excited about, because it will often dominate the conversation.

One more thing: it's important to connect with your audience. My problem (or, rather, my vendor's problem) is that I don't follow sports, I don't hunt, and I love my wife implicitly. I have shut down a number of vendors who come in, assuming none of those three things are true in an effort to 'connect' with me.

While connecting *is* important, it can be tricky to do. Remember that not everyone is stereotypical. Everyone is not you.

Hint #10: Eye contact.

Engage in constant eye contact throughout your conversation. Don't fidget, don't slouch, and keep your demeanor engaged and locked on target.

Inflatable Gorillas,
'Wacky Waving Inflatable Arm Flailing Tube Men', And You

For decades, these insane gimmicks have found themselves outside of, or on top of, business establishments as 'attention getters'.

Why?

If you know what I'm talking about, then they work. And *that's* why.

Often, businesses will add these ridiculous accoutrements to their exterior landscape as a means of letting the public know that something outside of ordinary business is occurring. Usually the event is a sale, blowout, markdown, going out of business, clearance, etc.

And as marketing tools, they do work. I know that I personally find the tube men almost hypnotic. They always manage to get my attention. Not because I love sales, but because I love the simple, elegant pneumatic mechanics of the things.

I'm a nerd. I know.

So you probably now find yourself saying, "Gorilla Marketing. Ha-ha, Heath – real funny, tongue in cheek, and all that.

Big deal!

What's so great about this idea?"

Here's what's great about it: I'm about to inject a dose of my patented insanity (possibly illegal in Tennessee) into it.

Ready?

What if you got one of the Gorillas and, throughout the course of the day, had a person in a banana suit running to and fro in front of the thing?

Or how about a guy in a Mario outfit running below it, with a girl in a princess outfit perched upon the roof above*?

*(If you don't get the reference, then just move on. You're probably good at sports.)

What if you got a pair of the tube men, and put them face to face in a mocked up boxing ring?

Or you could get both, and make the tube man appear to 'come out' of the Gorilla's butt.

That's right, I went there.

Whatever you do, consider that it's been done before. So what are you going to do about that?

Find an inexpensive way to unique-ify the thing, that's what!

Make it something different, insane, and memorable. And not only will folks pay attention, they'll most likely photograph the thing, and share it. Imagine your business in a viral photo marketing campaign that you didn't even know was happening.

I told you I wouldn't leave you hanging on this one!

Ooooooh! Shiny!

Make a decision! Hurry! Hurry, hurry, hurry, or... oops! Time's up!

Welcome to the land of the impulse buy, population: ever changing.

We as humans typically come complete with instincts (my personal jury is still out on the likes of Tonya Harding and Fiona Apple). We're born with an innate sense of understanding that that fanged critter that's twice your size and chasing you probably doesn't want to make friends. It's this 'fight or flight' reaction that often saves our butts when our conscious brain is on a coffee break or swimming in the *Tequila River*.

It is this innate sense of urgency that is an integral part of the impulse buy strategy. Marketing, at its core, is a concise manipulation of our emotions and feelings. From needing to feel 'cool' or 'in' by buying something, to calling something a 'limited edition', even if it is bathroom air freshener*. To be fair, *everything* – from atoms to the Universe – is a 'limited edition'.

*(That's a real example, by the way)

But how often do we parse that far into things?

Here's how the impulse buy works, in a nutshell:

You're faced, at the last possible moment before leaving a retail establishment, with a cadre of choices. The items are typically small, reasonably priced, serve a function, or are just plain tactilely or visually interesting. Our subconscious brain takes over, and begins running scenarios, often without our even realizing that it's happening.

"Does my breath smell bad?
Well, I did have that onion and limburger sandwich for lunch..."

"Ooooh - shiny!"

"That looks squishy – I need to touch it!"

"You know, I DO need more beef jerky in my diet."

"I'm thirsty, and I didn't even realize it!"

"Are there really 101 ways to please my woman?"

"What's Tom Cruise up to, these days?"

I could go on (and, frankly, would like to because I'm amusing myself at the moment) but I won't.

You get the point.

The angst and fear is further preyed upon in these situations by 'limiting' the time you have to decide. Often (but not often enough for me, thank you) you're in and out in a jiffy. So timing is everything.

And you know what?

More often than not, we allow ourselves to fall prey to this simple tactic. If you don't believe me, then start paying more attention to your last few moments in the store for a while. Then come back and tell me I'm wrong. I'll be here, waiting.

So now that we've taken the first step – admitting there's a 'problem' – how do we 'solve' it?

We 'solve' it by allocating space in your place of business for impulse items.

Sounds simple, right?

Not by a long shot. Your space is, most likely, limited. Which means that you need to squeeze every nickel you can out of every inch within your establishment. So you need to be fussy about what you choose to place in the impulse areas. Here are a few insights:

#1) The weirder, the better: If I've never seen it, or it does something wacky or inane, I'm going to be curious. And – for some reason – I always want to buy whatever it is for someone I know, or for some other genuinely stupid reason. As an example, I can tell you that a local vendor recently had a line of 'limited' owl-design cooking timers. I don't need a cooking timer (I have one built into my stove that works just fine), I do like owls, but the colors would never have gone anywhere in my home décor.

Want to know what my first reaction was?

"I need one of those! Those are amazing!"

I can't even begin to explain the phenomena. I'm still trying to fight the urge to go and buy one.

#2) Color-splosive and bling-tastic: If it's shiny, colorful, or – better still – an obnoxious combination of the two, then, like a fish to a fishing lure on a sunny day, humans seem to be drawn to it. They want to touch it.

#3) Serve a purpose: This one is a bit more boring, but not necessarily less profitable. If the item serves a purpose (and an immediate one is better) then it qualifies as a good impulse item.

#4) People are people: They need to eat and drink. And often, they'll keep doing it even when they don't actually need to. Fudge, candy, soda, and the like are all hard to resist. If you do go with a food item, you may want to find an 'accessory' item that offers a commensurate smell: a candle, air freshener, etc. to get the brain in the mood for purchase of the item. In fact, the closer to the entrance you get this thought planted, the better off you'll be come time to check out.

#5) Useless Novelties: I really want to explain why something that does nothing more than sit there and be itself, serving no other function whatsoever, sells. But I can't. They just do. Roll with it.

#6) Even e-stores can offer impulse items: Just add the appropriate coding to the site, so that 'random' or 'impulse' items pop up right before checkout is completed. Use buzzwords to make the buyer feel like a deal is being had (even if it's not a SUPER deal) and make it pleasing to the eye, yet simple enough for the average brain to parse out.

In the end, you can change it up periodically (and at the very least, with the seasons) to see what moves and what doesn't. If folks are drawn to it, but don't buy it, then consider understanding what got them that far, and seek a different product that gets them over that final hurdle.

Impulse stock is never an easy thing to divine. But if you take the time to experiment, do your homework, find something unique, and know your customers, then you can achieve success. And a little extra profit.

You're Never Too Old - Or Too Young - To Consider Adoption

You're driving along in your moderately priced sedan. It's a sunny day. You're on a country road. There are birds in the trees, the breeze is up, and life is good. Suddenly, something grabs your attention. It's coming up on the passenger side of the road. Oh! It's a blue/green/white/red/other colored sign!

"I wonder what it says?" you say aloud, to no one in particular.

As you draw nearer (all while minding your driving, and doing the speed limit or less, of course) you come to the realization that the sign indicates that some good soul(s) has/have taken on the thankless task of making this drive just that much nicer for you today.

How?

They've adopted this road, in an effort to keep it neat and tidy (because there are a lot of jack-holes out there who never learned that specialized receptacles for waste do, in fact, exist). Their reward is this sign that lets the world know that said person/group/company cares about their community.

Isn't that a nice thing?

Personally, I think it is. When a large corporate empire does it, I just feel like they're phoning it in by 'asking' their already (probably) oppressed employees to give up some of their free time to merit extra brownie points for a C.E.O. that they will probably never meet and who could be (for all they know) an evil cat in a cave somewhere in Tibet running the whole operation, bent on world domination.

Wow that was a long sentence.

But when a small, local company or entity does it, I realize that it takes some actual effort on their part. And it tells me that, no matter what someone might otherwise say, they actually care about their community.

Who knew that a little sign could say so much to me?

Not only does it tell me this, but every time I drive by it, I am reminded of that business. It's a branding dream come true.

So look to your local prefectures/towns/cities/counties/etc. to find out if strategic avenues in the vicinity of your business are available. And if they are, consider taking on the challenge of adoption!

Can't find one in your vicinity?

Consider asking another participant to switch with you. The worst they can do is say no.

Finally, if one *is* available, but it isn't a good locational fit, that still doesn't mean that you can't do it, or that you won't benefit from it. You could tout your business as a 'proud participant' in this green movement, while still gaining eyeball time. So don't discredit it out of hand.

Your Ticket To Big Profits Begins Here

What if I told you that you could sell a $100.00 item for $200.00, or more?

And what if I also told you that you would make the buyer ecstatic?

I'll wait until you're done making fun of me for being a nut job, unless you're clever. Then congratulations! You've figured out this section early. Consider me as having given you a gold star on your forehead.

Don't worry, though. I didn't lick it.

Probably not, anyway.

With that now done, let's bring everyone equally into the fold, shall we?

To make the above happen, you only need to familiarize yourself with one word: raffle. The concept of the raffle is old - really, *really*, old. In fact, it's pre-Biblical.

The concept is simple: one takes something of value, and affords all participants an opportunity to win said thing of value at a drastically amortized* cost, with minimal investment. With this in mind, here are some suggestions to make your raffle a success:

*(A word which literally means 'to kill off over time', by the way. How weird is that?)

First: Check your local laws and restrictions. In some places, raffles could be construed as gambling or a game of chance (which they pretty much are). So make sure it's legal!

Second: Make the buy-in amount small enough that folks feel like they'd be foolish not to get in on the action. I suggest a dollar. It's a nice round number, most folks won't miss it, and it doesn't force you to monkey around with change.

Third: Make sure the rules are clearly written, and clearly displayed. This way, no one is angry or 'surprised' by the outcome – you already covered that in the rules. And make sure to post the name of the winner in plain sight for a respectable period of time after the fact, so that no one suspects foul play.

Fourth: Employees and their families are not allowed to participate. You might be tempted to eliminate this oft-used clause, reassuring yourself that there's no harm in it: DON'T. Don't even think twice about it. Just hold fast on this point. If you want to maintain credibility, then heed my advice.

Fifth: Make the prize something universally desirable. If your prize caters to a niche market, then your whole store had better do so as well. Otherwise your interest – and participation – will be abysmal.

Sixth: Give yourself plenty of time to ramp up profit before the drawing. If you have twenty customers a day, then don't give away a $100.00 item in a week's time. Do the math, and err on the long side. But don't make the mistake of waiting so long that participation in your next offering becomes dissuasive. I recommend something once a month. See how it goes from there.

Seventh: Prepare for failure. If it doesn't work, then at least you've tried. But don't give away a car or some other outlandish thing that you can't afford to take a loss on. This is an experiment, after all, and will vary in success from business model to business model.

Eighth: Push the raffle. Gently – but push it. Make up posters, flyers, etc. Add mention of it to your web site and social media sites. Encourage folks to tell their friends, etc. If you have decent prizes, and good odds, then folks may eventually make a trip to your store to enter the raffle a monthly necessity.

And how great would *that* be?

Ninth: Consider a 'donated' prize. Perhaps a local business not directly in competition with your own would appreciate the opportunity and exposure that your business might afford them during the raffle period. They get advertising in a new/different market, and you're not out anything for the prize. Just make sure that – again – it's not something weird and completely dissociative. For example: a 'Live Varmint Removal' gift card from *Redneck Hank's Pest Control* in your Wedding Dress shop. Sure, it's hilarious but... all right, I'm still laughing. Maybe there's some merit to that example.

Let's move on.

Tenth: Make the raffle entry as simple as possible. Most folks like a tear-off ticket. Me, I'm partial to something more informative.

How about a slip of paper where they put their name, and e-mail address in a couple of empty fields?

This counts as their distinctive 'ticket', and also affords you an opportunity to mention that any e-mail addresses submitted may be used to let them know about promotions, etc. down the road. Now you're getting a two-fer out of the situation.

Eleventh: Don't assume that the prize has to come from within your stock. Perhaps a toy or game is the hot ticket in town. Find one, buy one, and raffle that off. Whatever brings in that extra revenue need not come from within.

In the end, Raffles are only as successful as you make them. It takes some work, a whole lot of consideration, and a little luck to make it a good profit model. When done well, and done correctly, they can be a great enhancement to business and profit.

Compare Your Way To More Sales

Since within these pages I seem to be on a 'stuff with shopping in the title' kick, I wanted to touch on something you've probably all seen done, but never considered doing yourself: comparison shopping.

What is comparison shopping?

Have you ever been in a store, and seen a person with a clipboard and other accoutrements in the seat portion of their cart, who seem to stare at all the items, make notes, and never buy anything?

Then you've spotted the elusive 'Comparison Shopper'*.

*(And, if I knew the Latin name, this is where I would deposit it in the monologue, just to show off).

They're sent to rival establishments to get a feel for pricing on similar or same items. They also test the atmosphere (not literally) and feel of the competition. They seek out intelligence on unannounced sales, specials, clearances, and on and on. To put it mildly, they're the enemy spy in plain clothes.

Being a huge fan of Sun Tzu's masterwork *'The Art of War'* (not to be confused with the lesser known, *'Zapp Brannigan's Big Book Of War'*), I always remember the gist of all the lines that center around knowing one's enemy as thyself. Basically, this is an ancient genius telling you to keep a sharp eye on your competition, but doing so from the grave in a translated form.

OoOoOoOo - spooky, I know!

Why am I spewing all of this?

In order to ask you this question: have you ever considered comparison shopping?

Now, hear me out. I know that a great many of you are local, small business owners. Many of you, in fact, may have no *specific,* direct rivals in the area in which you conduct business. Or at least, you don't *think* you do. I'm betting that those of you who believe that last statement are, in fact, wrong. There may be a few exceptions, but I doubt it.

Here's what's strolling around my brain at the moment. Many of you compete with stores offering *similar* items, stores that offer more commercial versions of your items, or stores that offer the same things (especially you folks in the service industries).

So why not take full, legal, advantage of the vast amount of data you can glean from their establishments?

For instance: why not take weekly, monthly, etc. trips to their venue to have a look around.

Are they selling incidentals or impulse items that would work in your store?

What specials or promotions are they offering that you could modify to fit your business model?

How does their store feel?

How does it smell?

Who are the primary clientele?

How is the lighting?

Are they discontinuing something?

If so, will someone tell you why?

What are their employees like?

Does anyone seem miffed, confused, or lost in the place – and, if so – why?

In the end, there is a *ton* of great information you can take in with all six of your senses... oh, sorry: five. I forget sometimes that you're not all psychic. Take a trip, scout the competition, and learn from their actions and movements. You have nothing to lose, and everything to gain.

And if you find them doing it to you, remember that all is fair in love and war.

Advertise Your Place, Mat!

Ah, the placemat. Oft home to scenes of Italy, maps of countries you've never been to, and the ever-popular maze or other child's entertainment.

Sometimes, however, they carry advertising. And this is where this idea comes in.

What if some of that advertising was for *your* business?

How, you ask?

Read on!

Here is what I propose:

If you want to try this sort of advertising, find a restaurant that uses the place mat in a daily fashion (and not the pre-fabricated, bulk ones or the laminated jobbies – you're out of luck on those). Contact the owner, and ask if you could advertise on the place mats, in exchange for offsetting some of the costs of having them printed. If they have a savvy business mind, they'll immediately see dollar signs. I know I would.

Conversely, you could find a restaurant that doesn't use place mats, and offer to provide them in exchange for being the sole advertiser on them. If you do pursue this, they'll need incentive. I'd suggest having stuff for kids to do on them, so as to provide an added value to the owner of the restaurant. And if worse comes to worst, you could offer a monthly 'fee' to them for the privilege, or a 'referral' bonus for customers who come from this vein of marketing.

It's not a slam-dunk, but it's also not something to walk away from without at least considering.

Be Vocal - Shop Local

Remember the days of shopping local?

Long before the advent of retail mega-chains, mega-malls where you can do everything from get married to buy a new muffler, local chain stores, and the *Sears* catalog, shopping local was the only way to get anything in real time*.

*(All right, some folks traded with peddlers, but I'm still counting that as local - work with me conceptually here, will you?)

Today, shopping local is still a viable option. Sadly, it's slowly trending toward extinction. It's not dead yet, though. And, with your help, it may just see a little bit of a resurgence.

So why is shopping local important, and how does it tie in with Guerrilla Business?

I'm ever so glad that you inquired!

First and foremost, shopping local puts you in contact with a real person who knows about the store or product. Often, they are the individual who made the item(s), or ordered the item(s) for their stock. Further, many local stores offer an amalgam of local wares under one roof, which further supports local artisans, crafts-persons, and cottage industries in your area.

That being said, engaging these individuals in conversation can not only give you more information about the product(s) or service(s) you desire to buy, they may also provide you a new, viable outlet for sales in your locale or region (i.e. – they may agree to sell your product for a cut of the profits). If nothing else, becoming a 'regular' of these venues, and befriending the owners or proprietors, can get your business name out there.

For example: we at *Digital Ninjas Media, Inc.* try to support local vendors. I'll be honest in saying that we don't do so in every case.

Why not?

Well, sometimes it just isn't good fit. Even so, we still attempt to play an active social role in commiserating with other local business owners. Sure, the vendor or owner may have no need of our services. But if we strike a friendly chord, perhaps sending business their way when we may, then they may be so inclined as to do likewise with their customer base. That's a whole new customer base. And it's a base who will be, more often than not, local, often befriending the owner or proprietor (that's you!) as well, and becoming a walking advertisement to their friends and family on your behalf.

Sound confusing?

It's really not.

So as the old adage says, "Be vocal – shop local!" It benefits your community, others within it, and possibly yourself as well.

Awww, Isn't That Cute/Sexy/Powerful/Intriguing?

You need a mascot.

All right maybe not.

At least consider the possibilities, though.

For the better part of one and a half centuries, companies have been utilizing fictional characters to hawk their wares as a means of gaining brand recognition and allowing continuity and synchronicity in their product offerings.

Try this: Toucan Sam, Speedy, Ronald McDonald, Tony the Tiger, Gecko.

My guess is that, as you read each one, you knew *exactly* which products they represented. Not only that, but I'd be willing to bet that your brain 'flashed' a picture of them in your mind's eye.

Now, try this: that guy who told that water cooler joke, a lemur, two tires rolling, a dude fishing.

Doesn't really compare, does it?

You might be surprised to find that in recent years, products that had once abandoned their mascots for decades have now elected to return them to the marketing fold.

To me it's a no-brainer.

A mascot is something that, when fictional, can be manipulated more effectively and with a greater level of variety than a simple run of commercials featuring real people.

Further, fictional characters don't disappoint you, don't cost a lot to hire, and never look bad on camera.

Have I got you thinking now?

Many of the companies that have not only survived, but thrived, in adverse conditions had mascots tied into their branding initiatives.

Think it isn't true?

Where would *Keebler* be, without those elves?

The answer is, "Who cares - the elves are an American institutional icon!"

Even small businesses can, if executed correctly, benefit from the use of a mascot. The biggest caveat is coming up with one, and then being committed to sticking with it as it becomes a figurehead for your local brand.

It's a downhill roll, so make those first choices and appearances count!

'Merger' Is NOT A Four-Letter Word

Business is hard - really, really hard.

A huge percentage of Americans have the opportunity, at least once over the course of their lifetimes, to go into business for themselves in one form or another. From direct-marketing sales to global corporate juggernauts, we all have opportunities in this country that many others in this world simply do not.

That being said, once the plunge (read - huge risk) is taken, it can be a fight to keep what you've poured your heart and soul in to. Many times, businesses fail because they're extremely adept at doing what they do (think attorneys), but are terrible, horrible, awful business managers (think attorneys).

Why?

Well, because they didn't go to school for business management and HR, did they?

They went to become attorneys. Asking them to be great managers is like asking an HR specialist to practice law.

And we'd never ask that of them, would we?

Likewise, most business owners face this 'many hats' dilemma. Some excel under the thumb of the challenge, while others curl up in a fetal ball in the corner, close their eyes, and rock themselves, thumb in mouth, until the nice young men in the clean white coats come to take them away.

(Ha-Ha!)

>Ahem<

To my untrained eye, there's a lot to be said for mergers. If a business can find a symbiotic partner to merge with, it often yields a mess (I am a realist, after all). But sometimes it yields something far more powerful.

I'll give you an example:

I run a machine shop. I don't own it, but I run it. When we were still in our infancy stages, we rented our unused building space to a small metal fabrication company. It was founded by a fellow and his wife. He was an expert in the field, and she was a smart, savvy woman who could manage a business.

After a few years of controlled growth, they were offered an opportunity to merge with a local machine shop. In the end, they did just that.

And where are they now?

Their respective businesses are symbiotically thriving under the umbrella of the single business model.

Better still, it allowed the expertise of the fabrication shop owner to be tapped further by using the significantly larger capital of the *other* business to implement a massive powder coating line (something he knew much about, but could ill-afford to implement on his own). It's one of the largest in the state. This only occurred because the merger brought together two halves of a potential whole. They're still happily doing business, and growing in a controlled manner to this day.

Granted, this might be cited as an exception. Nevertheless, it's a solid example of how a merger can make something new out of two existing things.

Don't think this applies to you?

Think again.

What if you are a local retail store?

Let's take *Culture Shock*, a local enterprise in my neck of the woods run by some of my friends. They run an indie record/vinyl music store, which also sells unique and hard to find items that appeal to the late-teens to early-thirty-something set. They possess a deep commitment to shopping local, and tapping local resources.

What if they could, somehow, merge with a coffee shop?

One business would symbiotically feed customers to the other. It's all hypothetical, but you can at least see the thought process behind it.

Likewise, even direct-marketing sales representatives can merge their resources into something more. What if a *Pampered Chef* Representative combined forces with, say, a *Tupperware* representative (again, I'm winging it here for the sake of example). They could share bookings, and sell things that appeal to the same audience to a group that they may not otherwise be able to reach.

I realize that this is all a bit glib. But, for me, this book is more about getting your *own* creativity flowing, and forcing you to think outside the box (pardon the cliché).

My creativity is already doing just fine. I wake up most days, looking at the box on the distant horizon. So feel free to ignore my examples.

Their Bust, Can Be Your Boom

It's inevitable: In the world at large, businesses fail. Sometimes it's timing, other times it is location, and once in a while it's simple ineptitude (okay, more than once in a while. Some folks just shouldn't be allowed to have discretionary money in voluminous quantities).

If the business that goes belly-up is in your field, then you're in luck. I know that sounds cruel, but let's be realistic. That's one less proverbial bear in the cage. And now, their customers will obviously come to you.

Wait - won't they?

Maybe - but, then again, maybe not.

If you want to tilt the odds in your favor - and I mean *really* tilt them - you have to do the unthinkable. You need to contact the business owner(s) of the business that is no longer in service. Hopefully, you haven't had a raging rivalry over competing yarn sales over the years that ended in shouted words about each other's mothers. If you have, then this probably won't work.

Here's what I propose:

Lovingly, and gently, contact the former owner. Let them know who you are, and that you're sympathetic. And if you're not, you should be. It could just as easily be you on the other end of the telephonic transaction. Be respectful, and mindful of their psychological pain.

Remind them that they had customers. They may not have had a lot of them, but they had them. This is where it gets touchy. Ask them if you can somehow acquire those customers. This can be done (if you're on good terms) by simply turning over a mailing list or e-mail file.

My advice?

You need something that they have, that still has value. Treat it as such. Offer to pay them a one-time fee for the list. Or offer to pay per conversion of customers who come over to your side of the fence.

A little more convoluted, but possibly more lucrative to them, would be to offer them a percentage of profits achieved from that client or business for a period of time. I don't recommend doing this if you're not good about keeping meticulous records.

Me?

I'd offer the one-time buyout.

In the end, if you approach this in the correct, loving, and compassionate manner (and for God's sake, you had better be sincere), they may see an opportunity to make one final profit from their now defunct business.

Worst case scenario?

They say no. At a total cost of $0.00 to yourself.

Part 4: Marketing

Strategic Offense & Smart-Bomb Marketing

Choose your prey (i.e. – potential customers) and then attack them (i.e. – market to them) where they live (i.e. – where they like to hang out and congregate.) All right – enough with the 'i.e.' stuff.

Why not leave a targeted, niche-specific, flyer for your business, services, or web site at niche hot-spots?

By targeting a specific market, you're sure to pique some interest in what you have to offer. And you can continue to frequent those places – again and again – to target new eyeballs, or remind the old ones that you still exist.

Opt-In Marketing

No one likes spam (the e-mail – not the canned meat product).

But how do you get your message out?

Try a soft-sell technique called 'opt-in' marketing. It's a long sell, but it's a better choice than cramming your business down some unwilling consumer's throat.

How does it work?

It's fairly simple. Offer interesting and useful facts, via social media or Blog, (sort of like I did when blogging the entries that later made up a portion of this work).

Soon word of mouth gets around, and people are coming to you!

Keep them interested by offering something useful. When the time comes that they need something, guess where they'll go?

And imagine how many folks each person knows, networks with, and is related to?

If your information is good, the world is your oyster. Sure it takes time and effort, but in all my years of experience in the world at large, I've learned that customers are, when treated to good service and value, exponential via word of mouth.

Cross-Pollination Marketing

'Cross-pollination' marketing is a great way for you to 'tag-team' with another business by offering a reciprocal presence. Find a vendor or company who does something similar enough to you to be relevant, but not close enough to be competitive. This way, you can each send business the other's way.

Or better still: offer to perform the service for the prospective client in need, outsourcing it, without them knowing that you personally aren't doing it (we loving call this 'farming a job out'). This is a little more risky, so make certain that you trust the other party who will be performing the actual work. I've seen this work in my world of precision machining, and I've also proven that it is a profitable way to add value to one's bottom line.

In my personal experience, I've noticed that when you offer great service, pricing, and communication (all of which the company I run does), customers are more willing to give you this sort of 'non-niche' business.

Why would they want to pay an inflated price (i.e. - inclusive of your mark-up percentage) for something they can go elsewhere for, though?

Essentially, you're charging them to be the bearer of responsibility in the situation, while allowing your superior services to be at their disposal, rather than their needing to deal with a second contractor who may not be as forthcoming. This has a value.

There is also value in time saved in shopping the job around, or seeking a contractor who has the capabilities required to complete the task. Here, we also sell our knowledge of these resources at a premium, by taking on the job. The customer has no notion of where it is being completed. All they know is that it is being done, and they need not worry because we're as communicative as they wish us to be, and will deliver as promised, at a bid price that is acceptable to them.

In fact, we have more than two dozen specialty shops who perform services that we cannot do in house, each year. The profits of this logistical enterprise, while small in comparison to the larger whole, have still become quite significant. Because we've developed this system, we are permitted to reap the rewards for handling the logistics, developing the vendor base and contacts, and taking on the added responsibility. Our unspoken motto has become, half-jokingly, *'Let us do your freaking out for you.'*

The result?

The customers are often eager to take us up on our offer.

So before you consider discounting this idea as 'not taking the moral high road', consider all of these facts - because they truly do have value. And that value is something that customers are often willing to pay for, even if you're not directly providing the service.

Guerrilla Branding: The Holy Grail Of Marketing

When was the last time you purchased facial tissues?

Soda crackers?

Made a copy?

Well, if you're like me (and God help you if you are, because my brain is a scary place), you buy *Kleenex*, and *Saltines*, and you *Xerox* things.

What's the difference?

The marketing is so well engrained into those products that their name has become not only synonymous with the product, but a ubiquitous moniker of it as well.

So how do you make this work for you?

First, and foremost, you need something simple and catchy. Once you've found your moniker of choice, add it to your advertising and correspondence materials. Ideally, you choose something whose ability to ease into a synonym for the product is a simple transition.

What do I mean by this?

I mean that if you choose, say, the name of a Mayan king it might sound cool, but it could be hard to pronounce, and not play well as a cat food brand.

♫♪ This Brand Is Your Brand ♫♪

As we've touched on above, guerrilla branding is a phenomenal avenue to continual marketing success. The biggest problem is that it's an avenue that can be more difficult to navigate than the Illinois Toll system on a moonless summer night in the rain while construction zones are in play.

For those of you who don't recall (I'll assume you have the attention span of a gnat, aren't reading this book in any sort of order, or went on a cruise just after reading the last entry), let me re-hash for a second: guerrilla branding is the phenomena of marketing an item that, over time, becomes synonymous with your brand.

Examples are *Xerox*, *Kleenex*, *Jell-O*, and *Saltines*. They've become synonymous with - or in some cases - eclipsed making copies, facial tissue, gelatin, and soda crackers.

One of my more recent clients mentioned to me in passing that she was considering developing a brand of product unique to her business, for her exclusive sale. In fact, while doing so, she mentioned to me a fact that few people know, but we had both learned over the years: many products that we purchase daily are manufactured in one place, and then re-branded to be sold in varying outlets.

For example: at one point in time, I was told that all of the standard, powdered, coffee creamer – regardless of the brand name it was sold under – was made by one company, and then repackaged by a number of others, under differing product names. I have no proof of this, but on some levels I could see it being true. And this, in my limited experience, is not a singular, unique example.

In cases such as that, it's *all* about the branding.

So how does this work for you?

First off, I would encourage you to close up your store or shop for the evening. If you don't have a physical storefront, then go to your work area. Have a nice cup of tea. Maybe a cookie – or even two – I won't tell. Then, take a good look around you.

What do you see?

More specifically, is there something around you that you can produce, purchase with re-branding, or a combination of the two?

Now close your eyes, and mentally go over your inventory, with the same thought in mind.

Some of my readers will bow out right about here because it either doesn't apply to them, or they're already doing it. I don't blame you one bit: there will be another time when a later entry will pertain to you, I promise.

Thanks for your continued readership – I appreciate it!

Now for those of you still reading, let me give you a real-life example from a new friend I made recently. This young woman began with something simple and time-tested: the sock monkey. Then, she amped it up to 11, stepped outside the box, and went guerrilla.

Her idea?

She created a line of unique, often one-of-a-kind, sock dolls (neé - veritable action figures) that were anything but ordinary, and far from traditional. Her company is named, '*Socks That Rock*'. It's a product that's fairly untapped, and she had the prescience to attach a name that is easy to remember, fun to say, and rolls off the tongue nicely. This is the sort of thing that I'm talking about.

Likewise, other readers of my blogs have come up with, or mentioned, store-branded hair coloring solutions, confections, edibles, etc. All are good ideas, and all are going to go far if the quality is right, and the branding is consistent, meets the criteria outlined above (easy to remember, fun to say, and rolls off the tongue).

So what are you waiting for?

In my experience, opportunity rarely knocks. Quite the opposite: usually you have to track it and subdue it, much like Arnold Schwarzenegger did with the offending alien in "*Predator*".

Get going, and get branded.

Part 5: The Internet And Social Media

Fishing, Weird Uncle Pete, And You:
What You Need To Know As A Business Owner

It all begins with *Facebook*. Pundits over the past few years have spoken openly about The Internet not being a place, but rather a medium. *Facebook*, it turns out, is one of the 'places' that the medium of 'The Internet' provides us. It does so for both our own personal enjoyment, and also our business venture's use as well. It continues to grow, evolving into something more phenomenal and varied by the month. For the moment, it is *THE* springboard, killer app* for small and cottage business.

*(At least, in my opinion.)

When my wife and I, as well as our business partner, formed *Digital Ninjas Media, Inc.*, we decided to attempt a guerrilla marketing thought experiment via *Facebook*. We hyped and hinted for more than a week, but never once specifically told anyone what we were up to. By the time we made the formal announcement about our new business venture, we had proven that outside-the-margins marketing was something that we could be adept at. The frenzied individuals spoke volumes.

What we hoped for this business to be able to achieve was this: we wanted every business owner – large or small – to have the services and expertise of a full-blown marketing and advertising firm at their disposal on an a la carte basis. This would allow them to utilize only the facets of what we had on offer that were relevant to their needs, and to do so with maximum effect via our depth of unique and varied expertise and experience – all without having to hire a single employee to work a single hour on any of these types of projects.

Over the subsequent months, I noted that folks were all too eager to post their business, sales, information, etc. in a number of the Facebook-hosted marketing forums that I had subscribed to. Some were honest mistakes (folks misunderstanding the razor-thin focus of the forum, and inadvertently considering it a free-for-all), while others were just blatant plugs for their business, which they clearly hoped wouldn't be removed by the complacent forum administrators.

Often, the administrators would give the benefit of the doubt (and be more civil than I might have been about it) when removing the offending posts. Over time, however, the civility gave way to overt frustration – and rightly so. I had watched these administrators weather far more than I would personally have. I have a low tolerance for recidivism, and an even lower one for stupidity.

Time and time again, they even went out of their way to point the 'wayward' offenders to the appropriate group for such things - specifically, local business advertising and booster groups. After seeing these 'other' groups mentioned a number of times, I finally took the initiative to pop over and take a look at them. And it was... depressing. Now, don't misunderstand: the fact that the group was there in the first place to meet those potential needs was great. The fact that very few were administered well, and worse still were used poorly, is where we'll jump off.

Over those months, I looked at all of those well-intentioned, but utterly failed groups. Over time, a pattern developed. The pattern was that there were either few, or zero, groups that functioned as desired, while also being administrated in a way that kept them humming. As these specific needs became apparent to me, I began to tailor brand new groups. These groups would cater to individuals with niche-specific or special needs.

Once in place, I developed an administration strategy (and found some volunteer administrators) to administer them in an overt way that was helpful, made the most of my and the other assigned administrator's specific areas of expertise, and above all wasted zero of the user's time.

In the specific case cited above (which was one of what would become almost twenty, to date), I created a *Facebook* group to specifically cater to this bunch of folks who didn't know where, exactly, to go to have their business voice heard. The difference, I decided, was that I was going to assist them – do a little hand holding - rather than just opening a virtual free-for-all graffiti wall and then disappearing like Jimmy Hoffa. The *Digital Ninjas: Business Billboard* group was born.

Advantageously, as new groups were created, I continued to precurse each of their named purposes with a '*Digital Ninjas:* ' moniker (i.e. - '*Digital Ninjas: Ask A Geek*', for example - a group that caters to computer, phone, and telecommunications users in need of free assistance by offering advice from more than thirty 'administrators' whose roots run deep in these fields, and some of whose day jobs are with *Fortune* 500 companies). This way, every time someone joined or used the group, they would have to remember who we were, as we offered them something for free to assist them with their needs, desires, and wants. That was the trade-off they had to endure. We had our names in their faces, they received free support.

Since its inception, the '*Ask A Geek*' group, in particular, has gone from assisting local friends and individuals, to also being a touchstone group for authors worldwide.

How?

This occurred predominantly through cross-posting in yet another group (developed by us) catering to authors wishing to escalate their relevance and peer base. Again, I saw an unfilled need, filled it, and now (thanks to my weird name, and tenacity) I am a known commodity to best-selling authors in all genres, all over the world. It's a pretty damn cool feeling, to be honest. It's humbling as well.

Back to the *Digital Ninjas: Business Billboard* group. Once the group was established, and the posts were flowing, I dropped in the first (of what would become dozens) of the cross-posted installments designed to assist cottage, small, and medium-sized business owners (found below).

Why?

To put it plainly, I had decided that everyone in our groups – regardless of why they were there, or whether they needed our services or not - deserved to be treated like a current customer. My thinking was that, someday, they or someone they knew just might become one. When, and if, that time came, I wanted to be there for them then as well; be the foremost consideration in their mind. It's worked – over and over again.

The very first post read as follows:

"What you need to know about advertising your business on a Social Media Group's wall. Any wall applies to what I'm about to tell you. Here's what you need to consider:

Advertising on a group wall, at its heart, begins as a losing proposition. Assume your message will go completely ignored. It's harsh, but if you expect the worst, you can better arm yourself to achieve the best. So before you hit that 'POST' button, consider this analogy I've cooked up for you.

When someone goes fishing, they do not take a stick, hook their belt to it, drop the end of it in the water, and walk away in the hopes that some astronomical odds will be in their favor that a starving, blind, stupid fish will eat said hook and hold on until they return.

No: most fishermen consider EVERYTHING. They begin with the type of fish they're trying to catch. They select the appropriate pole, and sometimes reel, for that type of fishing. Then they choose the strongest, least visible line to give them a further edge. They choose a well-made, well-considered, lure that is appropriate for their prey – sometimes based on the weather as well – and tie it on with a scientifically developed knot. But they're not done: Now, they choose an appropriate lake, and subsequent spot on the lake, to find the fish. Often, ridiculous numbers of electronics are brought to the party, just for good measure. And there's usually beer. I'm pretty sure that's so the fish have a little bit of a fighting chance.

Think about all of the thought that went into the entire endeavor before the first cast is lobbed. The fisherman has done everything he or she can do (or, at least, afford to do – fishing can be expensive, believe it or not) and NOW it's up to the fish.

"How is this relevant, Heath!?"

THIS is the level of preparation I want you to consider before you hit the 'POST' button. It sounds insane, but – believe me – it's that important.

Recently, I saw a post in one of our groups. I won't say for what, nor will I divulge by whom. What it said to me in the verbiage was this:

161

'I didn't care enough to tell you what I do, nor to spell this correctly, nor to punctuate or capitalize the sentence. I simply demand that you blindly appreciate what I'm doing, like my page, and buy something after YOU do all of the research into what I actually sell, and why you should buy it'."

At having first spotted the offending post, mentioned above, the marketing Nazi in me got a little upset.

Why even bother posting such a ridiculous nightmare? was my initial reaction, after having read the awful post.

Then, the compassionate side of my brain came off of its coffee break and said, "Did I miss something? I felt your heart rate go up drastically. Is Weird Uncle Pete around?"

Once the compassionate side sidled in and took the reins, I realized that this was an opportunity for me to gently teach, and hopefully share, some things that I've learned with others, in an effort to prevent them from making the same, catastrophic mistake.

So, as a phase-two, I kicked over to the web site that was posted as a link within the offending message. It was a blatant nightmare. Again, the products were all there, but there was nothing *compelling* at all. It was a rote list of items for sale, with names that vaguely outlined what the product might be, and that was it. In all honesty, I came away with little to no specific ideas about what most of the products might be for, as the names were more evocative of fashion than form or function.

Is this person ever going to make a sale?

I doubt it. In fact, I'd be surprised if anyone even took the time to follow the link. And this is where I want you to really listen: you might be the best widget maker/salesman/repairer/'other' around. But if you don't succinctly explain your product, in graduating levels of depth, then your chances of a sale are slim to none.

Your initial foray should be short. Intrigue the reader into wanting to see more. It should also be grammatically correct, and espouse correct punctuation. It can be funny, witty, insane, interesting – it's all good stuff, when done right. This is your proverbial bait.

Your second foray (what the user sees when they are interested enough to click through to your web site, *Facebook* page, or other medium) should also be succinct, well organized, and offer the opportunity for a third (and possibly fourth, fifth, etc.) level of information which are progressively more detailed.

If you just post, '*Here's this thing: $35.00*', then think about this: would you buy a thing in a picture with no description from someone who appears disorganized and whom you've never met?

If the answer is yes, then we totally need to talk because I want all of your money.

Oh! I'm sorry, where are my manners?

I want all of your money, *please*.

So do yourself a favor. Take the time to consider each progressive level of what you're offering; craft content that will make a distinct and lasting impression. Consider whether that little jumble of letters and punctuation will go out into the world to be the next millionaire-maker, or whether it will starve, homeless, under a bridge in some urban, death-maze metroplex. Because you work too damn hard in this life not to take every reasonable, legal, and righteous advantage that is available to you. The choice is yours."

That's how this book began. It's come a long, long way since those humble beginnings.

Unicorn Advice, Insurance Cults, And You

Already have a web site? Great! Already have a FAKE web site?

What?

You don't?

Well then, listen up!

Some of the most popular marketing movements in recent years have been viral ones. Even further, some were never meant to be movements in the first place. They just sort of happened. This leads me to an intriguing thought: why not develop a *fake* or *satirical* web site? And I don't mean something that *looks* like a web site. I mean something that *is* a web site, but also doesn't take itself seriously.

I can hear your confusion (or possibly there's a flying insect here in the office with me - it's hard to tell, the older I get). Let's create some fictitious examples: 'Consult A Unicorn'; 'Plumbing Tips With The Easter Bunny'; 'Hair Advice For Young Witches'.

See where I'm going with this?

If you can provide some insane content, your site may go viral. And the only one who won't have to pay to advertise on it is - oh, yes - you! Others may wish to, and this is where the site begins to pay for itself.

Let's be frank. Web sites are relatively inexpensive to host, if you have the acumen or ability to craft them yourself. The money part usually comes from creating killer graphics, interfaces, and content. This means you'll need to do a lot of the work from the get-go.

Can't do it yourself?

Consult someone who can, but lay out your expectations. Keep it simple, keep it simple, and keep it simple. This will keep costs down, and get you up and running quicker.

Even if you don't want to go whole-hog at first, you could, instead,

GUERRILLA BUSINESS ◆ HEATH D. ALBERTS

develop a 'sub-site'. This is a web page, on an existing web site, that LOOKS like a new index.htm page (the 'front page' of a web site) but is, in fact, a sub-section all unto itself. These will cost you NOTHING more to host, and might even be better for you, as it will be inalienably tied to the anchor page - YOUR page. A sub-site would look something like this in the URL:

http://askaunicorn.mitzispotholders.com
http://www.mitzispotholders.com/askaunicorn

Sound like too much work?

Can't tell a floppy drive from a USB port?

Alright, let's try another tactic in the same vein, then. What if you created a *Facebook* page devoted to something odd? For example, *'The Cult of Flo: the* Progressive Insurance *Girl.'* Yeah – it's crazy. But I can guarantee that someone will join. And others will follow if the content is sound, consistent, and resounding.

The biggest things to remember are that you're making a commitment of time that you had better consider beforehand. Likewise, your monetary resources may be tapped to some degree, and you need to make sure that anything you do falls into the 'approved' column – and follows all of the applicable rules of wherever, or however, you do it. Don't infringe on copyright, don't commit fraud, and don't do anything stupid like teach kids how to make Plutonium* in their kitchen.

*(But if you know how, you can totally send me an e-mail about it. I won't tell a soul - I promise!)

Have fun!

Be wacky!

And wield your creative license like a broadsword!

404 Error Pages: Be Positive About This Negative Phenomena

You've all seen them: those pesky *'404 Error'* pages that pop up just when you think you're going to discover the secrets of the universe, or see two hippos doing it.

But what in the world does that mean?

According to *Wikipedia*:

"The 404 or 'Not Found' error message is a standard, HTTP response code indicating that the client was able to communicate with the server, but the server could not find what was requested. A 404 error should not be confused with "server not found" or similar errors, in which a connection to the destination server could not be made at all. A 404 error indicates that the requested resource may be available again in the future."

Okay, so none of us are 100% perfect typists.

So why not capitalize on that fact?

Did you know that you can create and install CUSTOM 404 pages for your web site?

It's true!

So why not turn something inadvertent into a potential advertising bonanza. Here's how it works:

You create a custom 404 page (with the keen directions, found at: http://queenofsubtle.com/404/?page_id=2128).

Your customers, or someone else in the world at large stumbles upon it. It's freaking hilarious, poignant, or insightful because you've done your homework and crafted something memorable. Now you've turned a boring, irritating negative into a positive. In fact, if it's funny/clever/witty/informative/useful enough, it might even go viral.

And wouldn't *that* be something?

Podcasts: Your Ticket To Vocal Notoriety

First of all, for those of you who don't know, a PodCast is a digital, audio, 'broadcast' that is provided over the Internet either on demand, or by subscription. Typically, they are something that you look forward to. It might be a weekly radio program, topic- or interest-specific tips, songs from your favorite band, or news. Anything with content that is unique and/or desirable. Some aren't all that desirable, but that's just a matter of personal taste.

Two things that have changed drastically in recent years are the facts that more and more drivers own *iPods* (or other similar devices – I'm not prejudicial, just preferential), and more and more are commuting longer and further distances to their places of employment. Living outside of Chicago, I personally know a whole host of folks who live and die by their *iPod*, and audio books, to keep them sane on those long commutes.

I also know folks who text and talk on their phones while they drive. To those folks I say, 'Don't – it's dangerous'.

They'll come around. Especially as laws against doing so become more prevalent and enforced.

So what do you do that's PodCast worthy?

Can you offer hair and make-up tips?

Car advice?

A joke of the day?

A news snippet?

Poodles wailing in unison to the strains of hits of *The Backstreet Boys**?

*(Weird Uncle Pete insisted I put that one in – I'm not entirely sure why, and not sure that I really want to know, either. Also, Weird Uncle Pete has a fan page on *Facebook*, because I practice what I preach.)

Whatever it is, you can now become your own broadcast medium.

Here's an address to one of a number of helpful sites that take you step by step through the process:

http://radio.about.com/od/createyourownpodcast/ss/How-to-Create-Your -Own-Podcast-Make-Your-Own-Talk-Show-Music-Program-or-Audio-Strea m.htm

There are a great many more, so if this one isn't right for you, I would suggest using your search engine of preference to locate one of the myriad others available either for free, or commercially for a fee. There are also a few sites out there that cater to not only creating – but free hosting – of PodCasts. However, as of this writing, many are either gone, or on their way out, because the business model doesn't really lend itself to longevity in its current form. So I would strongly urge you to consider your options before you wed yourself - and your content - to one of those sites.

So go forth, and wield the digital pipeline to your own audio-based ends!

Pinterest: A Virtual Cornucopia Of Possibilities

I first heard about *Pinterest*, and the subsequent phenomena of it, in September of 2011. At the time, my sister-in-law and some friends of hers at work were hooked on this site. She had mentioned it to my wife in passing, which is how I first got wind of it. When I sat down to learn more about it, I put two and two together and smelled a potential winner. At this time, we were still ramping up for the official roll out of our new business venture. In fact, this was about the same time that I was developing the in-house, Intranet HTML 'Jump' page, chock full of useful links in marketing and virtual tool categories for use in the upcoming venture, and by future clients.

The next day I went to the site itself, only to find out it wasn't so easy to get in. You needed to apply, or have an invitation. I ended up applying. Unlike many thereafter, I was approved within a day or so. Which was a far cry from the 1-3 weeks I was still hearing about at the time I wrote this. Apparently, there was a line outside that was akin to that of a trendy nightclub.

And why not?

That, after all, is a well-worn marketing tactic unto itself.

If everyone could get in on a whim, would it still hold the same mystique?

Besides, at the time, it was also working like a charm for the public rollout of *Google+* (intentional or not).

Now, years later, I've come to understand that the weird issues I had with the site once I was 'in the door' were probably kinks in an imperfect system. So it appears that while the restrictions were in place to work the system up to full capability, they served a second purpose as a marketing tool. I have to believe that it was intentional because – well – it's brilliant.

Not familiar with *Pinterest*?

That's all right – you will be. Here's what you need to know:

Pinterest allows you to add an interactive 'P*in It!*' button to your browser of choice. When you find a photograph of something you like, almost anywhere on the web, you simply click the '*Pin It!*' button. You are then presented with a sub-interface that provides some categorization and customization choices. You are afforded the opportunity to categorize the 'pin' in any one of a number of pre-loaded, generic categories (defined as 'boards', in a manner akin to a bulletin board) – OR – you can design your own categories ('boards'). Finally, you are permitted to add a tagline/paragraph to the 'pin', explaining your thoughts on it in as much or as little detail as you care to impart.

Once the 'pin' is complete, it becomes a fixture on the respective 'board' that you have pinned it upon for both yourself – and your 'followers' - to see. It is also hyper-linked to the parent page from whence it came, should you or others wish to learn more about it, or revisit it.

Followers, you say?

Yep!

Pinterest allows you to 'follow' other pinners, and for other pinners to 'follow' you. So, hypothetically, you could develop a following if your pins are unique enough to warrant it. In fact, users are permitted to 're-pin' from your board to their own, if they find something they like. Based on the number of 're-pins' I receive, I think it's my writing style, and not the pin itself, that gets me re-pinned.

I'll be honest, I don't really get the draw. First, because *Facebook* actually allows you to do many of the same things (and if you don't know what I mean, then try fooling around with all those choices in those drop-down menus there, sometime). What it *doesn't* allow is the simplistic elegance that *Pinterest* provides. So that's a definite point in *Pinterest*'s favor.

As I followed the growth of the phenomena, I noticed a distinct pattern (at least, within my personal circles). That pattern is this: women, ages 23-45 seem to be the demographic that's eating this up. I have a number of highly intelligent, female friends who fall into this category. They're beyond addicted.

As a way to cover all of our bases, we at *Digital Ninjas* all agreed to utilize this site when we happened upon it, all those years ago.

Why?

Mostly for the reasons outlined below.

Want to know what happened?

My wife – the only woman in the group – loves it. And the remaining pair of us (both guys) don't get it, don't enjoy it, and don't get much use out of it.

In fact, in my case, I had to *force* myself to build up what I felt was at least a respectable site – all 100+ pins worth. And even that was a tough pill to swallow, because every moment felt like work. I still add something here and there, in the hopes that I will have a 'Eureka!' moment, and get hooked to a positive end.

But, so far?

Nothing.

So where do you fit into all of this?

Let me first say this: just because a new social media platform exists, doesn't mean that you have to be on it. In my opinion, there are just too many, and it will either kill you, or you'll end up abandoning it.

With that being said, *Pinterest* may very well be (or become) an important part of your social media marketing package or campaigns.

Let's review a couple of relevant angles:

1.) It's free! And free stuff, while not always good (i.e. – soiled mattresses or advice from Weird Uncle Pete), should always be considered.

2.) It has a significant following of regular users and it's still rapidly ascending in popularity. This means that if folks are spending time there, you might need to be at the party as well, to rub elbows, if you plan on making some new business connections of any sort.

3.) It can humanize you, or your business. You can soft-solicit things you find intriguing, important, etc. and potentially connect with customers, or potential customers, in this way. Perhaps they share interests, like things that are green, or lascivious photos of poodles. Whatever – it's another avenue for folks to get to know you, without compromising too much personal information.

4.) It can be a visual marketing tool. Your business could post 'before and after' shots, you could Pin (and cross-pin) your sites, or sites of allied vendors. You can show interesting hairstyles, products, and on and on – the possibilities are so myriad, that if you can't think of fifty, then you really need to lay off the weed, and at the very least switch to alcohol.*
*(I don't condone illicit use of either – I'm being funny here. Work with me.)

5.) Try it out! Check out your competition – are they using it? If so, how?

What ideas can you take away from their usage?

In the end, *Pinterest* seems here to stay in the American social collective consciousness. As a business owner, you should at least consider the possibilities it might hold for you - even if, in the end, it's not a good fit.

Increase Your Search Engine Relevance

Want to increase your ratings on search engines, but don't want to spend a penny?

No worries!

For starters, make sure that you've done everything that you can to Search Engine Optimize (or 'S.E.O.') your web site, in the form of meta tags, relevant first lines, organized content, etc. & so forth*.

*(If you want to know more, there are a huge number of searchable resources that are not only changing minute-to-minute, but are a lot more clear and concise than I wish I could be on the topic. So, I will reluctantly defer to their superiority in this instance.)

With that task complete, ask your friends and family to do the following: Choose the words or phrases found on your site that you would most like to be recognized as being associated with it. Have them enter it in their search engine of choice, and keep paging through until they find your page, then click it. Ask them to do it from their work, and cell as well, to maximize 'unique' hits, and also as often as they can possibly manage. At the same time, make minor changes as often as you can find the time. Even something as simple as the 'last updated' date on your index page can be of help in gaining ground in the search engine result listings. As of this writing, while no one but they themselves knows what arcane formulas drive the *Google* algorithms, it can be said that *Google* seems to like when pages aren't stagnant.

Free Business Listings Can Bolster Your Internet Presence

Want more exposure for your business?

Perform a web search for the term 'free business listing'. There are dozens of resultant places where you can list your business, in varying degrees and depth, for precisely ZERO dollars. Why bother? The more places you're listed, the more likely search engines will believe that your search relevance is higher. Not to mention the fact that it increases the likelihood of your potential customers being able to find you.

Plus, did I mention it's FREE?

I'm pretty sure that I did...

Google Analytics: Your Silent Partner In Marketing

Google Analytics is a free tool for tracking web site traffic. When attempting to utilize a marketing strategy, a business would do well to comprehend and understand their baseline numbers, so as to be able to quantify whether or not the tactic is functioning effectively. *Google Analytics* is (as of this writing) a free tool, and is relatively simple to use. There is even a tutorial, found on the *Google* site, as well as a number of *YouTube* videos that can assist a small business in understanding how to make it work for them.

Facebook Ads: Our Often Misunderstood Friend

Facebook is, at its core, a difference engine. It takes vast amounts of data and parses them out to the *N*th degree to allow advertisers the opportunity to laser-guide their advertising to a point that has been, heretofore, predominantly unimaginable.

This is where you – and your business – come in. It has been said that it requires as many as THIRTEEN TIMES for you to get in front of someone's eyeballs, screaming, "Hey! Look at Me! Look what I can do!" before they suddenly snap out of their advertising-induced coma and notice you. That being said, *Facebook* ads offer you an opportunity to choose not only your potential – or intended – viewership, but also your price point for doing so.

And that's where it gets a little tricky. Here's what my first experience was like:

In order to understand the thing, some explanation is in order. *Facebook* ads allow you to select a price that you're willing to pay for every individual that 'clicks through' your advertisement. If they don't click, you don't pay (as of this writing, anyway). Setting the price yourself is great, except that if you don't pay, you also don't get nearly as much exposure. On any given day, *Facebook*'s algorithm makes you aware of a 'suggested price range'. This is used to understand how many other advertisers are competing for the eyeballs that you're after. The higher the number, the more aggressive the other advertisers are. Over the span of the ad that I ran, it vacillated from as little as twelve cents, to nearly three dollars. Individuals willing to pay the higher price would have substantially more eyeballs.

How and why?

It's because of their willingness to pay a high price per click-through gives *Facebook* more incentive to push *that* ad far more than the others. In fact, if they haven't set a per day expenditure cap, it may be the *only* ad that is seen that day by those choice, potential customers. If they have set one, then once that cap is met, the next-highest 'bidder' per click-through becomes the new focus of *Facebook*'s marketing crush, and so on down the line.

In light of those facts, there is something to be said about not being too cheap on the price you're willing to pay per click-through.

I chose to really drill-down, in an effort to market my first fictional novel to an extremely limited market of specific individuals. I chose a median price-point, and had over 1,700 views, and 69 click-throughs, at a cost of just about $11.00 in total (I'm cheap when I'm experimenting).

The beauty of the thing?

1,700 people saw my ad, and I only got charged for the 69 of them that pursued learning more about what they were seeing by clicking-through the link. Or possibly, several hundred saw my ad several times – now I'm beginning to find a place in their mind – also a good pattern.

I then tapered the aforementioned, median price point back to something like ten cents per click through, and the views went waaaaaay down. But they still arrived, nonetheless.

Interesting, I thought.

The final result: I spent eleven bucks and sold zero books from that endeavor. Either it wasn't a good fit for my product, or I didn't target properly.

In conclusion, here's my advice: every business is different. Choose your core market – and only your core market – to target first*. Try shooting for a reasonable rate that fits both your budget, and your needs. Fair warning: the suggested price range often fluctuates wildly from hour to hour, and day to day. Don't panic. It *does* come down – often – if the selected group is 'tight' enough in scope.

*(Unless you're rich - then do whatever. And buy me something nice, while you're at it).

And feel free to play!

Choose two cents a click, and see what happens. You can fund that from your car seats, or couch cushions. And there's always that cost cap that you may set for maximum daily click-through costs, or for the open-ended duration of the campaign – but set it wisely.

An Aside, And A Little Reflection On An October Morning

I spent over two hours, one October morning, a few years back, seeking out Guerrilla Marketing blogs and articles. Specifically, I searched the term, *'Guerrilla Marketing Tips'*.

As I clicked the resultant links, I found that many were results that occurred in blogs which permitted interactivity with the originating blogger. I gave them all a cursory read.

Then, I went on the offensive. I developed a clear, concise response to a number of these blog posts as a post-able comment. I then posted wherever said comments would not seem out of place, and could potentially even do some general good.

What did I notice?

After about the fifteenth one, I found that I was seeing some order to the chaos of who, specifically, was commenting. Two or three individuals, in fact, had clearly done what I was doing – but that was all. On some of these pages, mine was the *only* comment that had been offered up in months.

So what does this mean?

It means that, like two of those folks that I hadn't heard of, someone might see my comment, like it, and then take the time to track *me* and *my business* down, as I did theirs.

Will it come to anything?

Who knows?

Was it worth the couple of errant hours spent listening to music and geeking on the web?

It's hard to say, but geeking and music are seldom in the 'time wasted' column, in my book.

Months later, I *Googled* myself (feel free to insert your own perverted joke here), and found that those responses had been found, cataloged, and subsequently tied my name into those business entities who were well established, and associated with marketing. So - by association - I had now gained some residual credibility, just for having written a short response.

Try it with your business, or your 'zone of knowledge', and see if a pattern develops. If it does, take note of who is doing what, where, and how the responses are being received. Then, take your moment to shine and offer up something useful, but also something that predicates an individual's desire to learn more about who you are, and what you do.

Infect The World - With Viral Video (Wait - What Did You Think I Meant?)

Let's take a moment to talk about a more and more consistent phenomena: that of the viral video. For those of you who do not know what I'm speaking of, here's a two-second lesson. Viral videos are those funny/cute/stupid videos that your Aunt Fran is always shot-gunning out to everyone in her mailing list, or that appear weekly on a whole host of video compilation comedy shows.

"Oh, *those*!"

Indeed!

Have you ever wondered how it was that those specific videos, above all others on offer, achieved such a level of popularity and renown?

If it isn't obvious, then here's the answer: it's because they're giving something away, without necessarily getting something in return. Which is all well and good for the hobbyist or random shut-in with a camera fetish and an Internet connection. But since you're reading this sagacious, and well-reasoned book I'm assuming that you are neither of these. I'm assuming, in fact, that you're in business to make money. I know that I sure am.

So, the question becomes, "How do I make this phenomena work for me?"

Track down a few of those videos that have stuck in your brain's memory banks. With that done, think of how you can create and present a video similar to that, or in a similar style.

For me, it's all about funny. I'm not about to risk my tuchus blowing myself up with airbags, surfing off of buildings, taunting dangerous animals, or shooting bottle rockets out of my teeth... again*.

*(Yep – I've done that last one. I don't recommend it.)

So my answer is to make something funny, but include advertising as well, front and center.

Currently, we here at *Digital Ninjas Media, Inc.* are in the process of writing, for ourselves, just such a webmercial. It involves a ninja whose training is no longer in demand, so she has to get a day job. We plan on making it silly, and something that you would feel compelled to show to those that you know.

And what will that do?

It will assist us with the ongoing war known as 'branding'. It will perpetuate – and virally disperse – who we are: The Wacky Gang at *Digital Ninjas Media, Inc.*

I would encourage you to noodle this over. Perhaps you could put together a how-to video, a music video, a skit, or some other interesting or insane piece of videography to tout – and further – your own business. This is especially relevant if you offer a product that is unknown but useful, or can offer some type of advice or tip that is not commonly found.

Meet Craig Newmark: Your New Friend In Advertising

For years professionals, pundits, and users alike have begged Craig Newmark to change the dynamic of his phenomenal creation. And for years, to both their astonishment and dismay, he has elected to politely tell them to 'cram it with walnuts'. Of course I'm paraphrasing, but you get the gist.

Don't know who he is?

Oh, yes you do!

Mr. Newmark is the founder of *CraigsList*. Since 1995, Mr. Newmark has provided an open and free forum for distributing information, goods, and services.

And this is your cue to make it advantageous with regard to your particular, self-centered needs. Take the time to study what's out there.

What headlines grab your attention?

What words are laser-specific to the market you wish to reach?

Then, figure out how and where best to post your message, followed by crafting verbiage that's poignant, intuitive, and fun.

It's free, so what have you got to lose?

Need Exposure Help? *YELP!*

YELP!

Oh, sorry – I didn't mean to frighten you, there. I'll say it more quietly this time.

Yelp!

For those of you who are already nodding then – congratulations! – you're riding the social media wave. For those of you who are waiting for the punch line, can't figure out what I'm talking about, or have heard this term before, but don't know what it is (beyond what your dog does when you step on him on your way to the bathroom at 3:00 am), then this section is for you.

Read on!

Yelp! is an on-line, searchable business 'bulletin board' that is rather unique among similar sites for several reasons. First and foremost, it allows a breadth and depth of information to be presented in an intuitive way to potential clients or customers that the other services that I've been exposed to just don't seem to quite measure up to.

Oh – and did I mention that it's FREE?

If not, then allow me to introduce incentive number two. It's free. Not only is it free, but it increases your exposure in a number of ways, not limited to further exposure on *Google* or other search engines.

In point of fact, it can function as a 'mini' web site. If you can't afford a real one of your own, it's a good 'next-best' thing. It's *that* broad in the amount of detail that it allows you to convey.

Not on *Yelp!* yet?

Well, there's no time like the present to branch out, spread your wings, and remind the world that you're there, you're selling, and you want their business!

One point of note before doing so, however: do it right. Take the time to make the best use of each of the offered categories by maximizing information in a comprehensible and compact form. Make the pictures count, and choose those that are both well composed and well lit. If you need to manipulate a photo to get it there, then I recommend that you do so. That is, of course, unless doing so leads to potentially false advertising. Don't skimp out on this because, like a science project in grade school, your efforts will be immediately identifiable. Spelling, grammar, content, data, visuals – all must present a phenomenal package to the potential client. They should speak to them in a way that says, "If we care enough to present this data in such a grand fashion, imagine what we can do for you/sell to you/do to you!"

Since the initial drafting of this segment, we've come upon a client who was heavily against *Yelp!* Curious, we inquired about the reason for this open disdain for what we felt was an amazing, free product.

The reason was that their *Yelp!* site received a horrid review that was ill-founded and proved to be completely false in nature. I was shown the data, and found that I agreed with their assessment.

I asked what they had done to rectify the situation.

They had gotten intimately involved with *Yelp!*, but the folks there remained stalwart in their permitting the review to remain. Freedom of speech won out, even in the face of clear evidence to the contrary.

Reviews are a double-edged sword. I have a 'troll' review on *Amazon*.com regarding my first novel. It persists to this day, because I'm bound by the end-user licensing agreement that I agreed to conform to in order to use their platform for my needs. Things like these could prove damaging to your business, in the long run, so make SURE you're really ready for potentially negative reviews (even false ones) because they will most likely not be removed. And before you sign or click, make sure you understand your rights when using those free services.

FourSquare: It's More Than Just A Game

What if I told you that your customers could advertise for you, in real time?

Don't believe me?

Well, you should, because it's true!

How, you ask?

Allow me to introduce you to *FourSquare*.

FourSquare is a connectivity and locational tool that is interactively connected to *Facebook*, as well as other social media services. It allows your customers to 'check in' at your place of business. This check in subsequently broadcasts to the pre-determined social media outlets that they have set it up for and – voila! – everyone who follows them knows where they are (or where they've been.)

Cooler still, *FourSquare* allows you to 'check' for other facilities in the immediate area that allow for check-ins: and one of those could be yours!

Here's a good example: the *Chili's* restaurant in my neck of the woods allows you to check in when in their confines. As a thank you, they supply you with a coupon code that, when your server is advised of it, lands you a free order of chips and salsa. They're willing to part with it to get you to let your friends know that you're eating there.

Here are the potential results of this: often times, friends will also be in the area, and come and join you for lunch. Other businesses in the vicinity are also recognized as check-in spots, offering premiums and promotions that are *FourSquare*-only. So when you're getting your chips and salsa, you will also find out that the *Office Depot* across the lot has a special on chairs, and the *PetSmart* two buildings over has a buy one get one free deal on goldfish. To me, it's a pretty amazing tool for randomized marketing.

And it works!

Know how I know?

Because even before I had a smart phone, my wife would let me know all of the above when we went to *Chili's*.

Another bonus?

FourSquare is F-R-E-E-free. So, if you have a physical storefront, you need to be accessible through this service. There's really no compelling reason not to be.

Fashion Exposure: Want More? Try Polyvore!

In the age of information sharing and the potential for humanization of local business owners to their desired clientele, sharing the right information in the right places at the right times can create more sales - with minimal interaction - than, in my humble opinion, at any other time in human history.

Businesses whose products center on fashion, accessories to fashion, or perhaps even grooming (i.e. - hairstyles, nails, etc.) may find interesting and new ways to connect with potential clients by using the fashion-interactive site known as *Polyvore*.

Polyvore (www.polyvore.com) was launched in February of 2007 and, made *Time Magazine*'s list of the *50 Best Websites for 2011*.

What does this mean to you?

In my opinion, *Polyvore* is a marketing medium that's ready to erupt on the social scene. It allows users a social outlet to build fashion 'sets' from images gathered from the four corners of the web. What the site gains is insight into what is trending hot and cold, and hard insight into where their client's collaboration and production monies would be best spent. The depth and nuances of the data has been reported to go into infinitesimally minute detail. Essentially, this changes the dynamic of the fashion industry from being dictatorial, to being democratic. The public's voice may now be heard, and drive the fashion industry toward their desired ends - and not the other way around.

Encouraging your clientele to use *Polyvore* may offer you insight into their needs, wants, and desires. It may also offer your personal lines of clothing, accessories, or services an opportunity to find a new market, as your clientele may be encouraged to include your product in their 'sets', for others to latch on to socially and - hopefully - result in more sales and exposure for your brand.

Part 6: Other Stuff You Should Probably Consider

There's No Accounting For Failure - Unless You Fail To Account

One area of your business that I strongly recommend you don't skimp on is the accountant.

Why?

For starters, a good accountant can save you money. Second, they can keep you on the right path with 'The Man', and keep you out of trouble. This is what they do for a living. The tax law in America is a proverbial nightmare, with page upon page upon nightmarish page of laws, revisions, statutes, limitations, exceptions, rules, regulations, sub-categories, arcana, and a lot of other nouns that I'll leave out. The bottom line is that you don't have time to keep track of it, because if you did then you'd be an accountant, and would have no time for *your* business. And if the word 'audit' doesn't strike fear into your heart as, say, the words 'herpes', 'pregnant', and 'cancer' do, then you really need to re-think your being in business in the first place. Trust me on this one.

A phenomenal mistake many make is choosing an accountant at random.

My advice?

Don't.

Choosing an accountant should be like choosing an employee - even more so, because you're entrusting them with the financial success or ruin of your business on a phenomenally large level. Getting referrals is good, but not good enough. The reality is most 'referrers' don't understand what they're referring when it comes to accountants. I've met accountants who have knowledge of tax law that would scare any normal mortal, but who wouldn't give me - the client - the time of day. This is great, but I - personally - need to trust and feel comfortable with the person holding my financial life in their hands. And being me, I appreciate reciprocal conversation now and again.

When I chose an accountant for our new business venture, I was sad to walk away from the firm that I had been using for personal returns for years.

The reason?

It was clear that while their knowledge was far beyond exceptional (and I willingly paid a premium for that breadth and depth of knowledge), their actions stated that I was not important to them in the slightest. And in the end, it bothered me enough to walk away from the sound and deep tax advice that they could provide.

I was on the hunt. I asked for referrals. As always, the kindness of others was my burden to bear. Most of the suggestions were well-meant, but poor ones. Then I received a sound one, from a trusted friend, who gave reasons and specifics. I made an appointment to sit down with him, and ask his opinions on matters that were important to me. After twenty minutes of speaking with the man, I knew he was for me. Of the few I considered, not only was he the most humanized and congenial, he also showed an aptitude for my needs, and surprised me when I learned that he was also on a local, social outreach board for businesses. We, in fact, had utilized the services of that very same board (it was free, and we felt that we had nothing to lose), and appreciated what they were trying to bring to small businesses in the area.

And that, as they say, was that. I had done my homework, asked for referrals, gotten to know the person behind the business, liked him, connected with him, and felt worthy of his time. He had answered my questions, offered excellent suggestions, and gave me pause when he considered angles and points that I had not. All in all, it was a lot of work. Yet when everything was said and done, I knew that I was in good hands - hands that would keep my financial path on the straight and narrow.

Can you say the same?

And if so, what makes you so sure?

Are you willing to bet a seasoned Auditor?

'Lawyer' Is *NOT* A Four-Letter Word

Let's be honest: most of us see lawyers in a negative light. They're often perceived as money-sucking fiends who want nothing more than to sue the pants off of someone, and then vie for their skin and hair as well. I'll be honest: when I was younger, I had a disdain for, and fear of, lawyers.

Apparently, some karmic re-alignment was in order, when my wife received her Paralegal Certification, and my brother - inexplicably - chose to become an attorney. And while my notions of others were easy to cement, having never actually known them, these two occurrences gave me pause because - well - I knew the offending parties, and they were pretty keen.

Over the ensuing (no pun intended, but...) months and years, I have been privileged to meet and get to know several attorneys. Some were in fact stereotypical. Most, however, were hard-working, genial folks who were genuinely concerned with the well-being of - yes, themselves - but, also, their clients. Since that time, I no longer see them in a negative light. In fact, truth be told, I now see them as a powerful asset to keeping me from meeting others of their kind, who want some of my money, because I have done something stupid.

You and, conjunctively, your business, should seriously consider retaining one. As stated in the case for accountancy above, it's a good idea to ask for referrals, perform interviews, and get comfortable with the purveyor of legal services. You might be shocked to know this, but all lawyers are not alike.

World changing, I know.

First, and foremost, make certain that the lawyer you choose specializes in the fields that you will require. If you need patent law, then an attorney who specializes in divorces probably isn't the best choice. That isn't to say that they aren't *capable* of assisting you - they probably are. But like the aforementioned tax law, the law-law is even more unwieldy, confusing, and counter-intuitive at times. It is often said that 'ignorance of the law is no excuse'. Cover your ears, if you don't like swearing, because I totally call 'bullshit' on that one. I don't think there's a human alive that has - or can - absorb the law. It is, in fact, a physical impossibility (okay, there might be some savant in the Ural Mountains or something who can - I can't know everything). The law is so voluminous, countermanding, and unwieldy that even lawyers - though they may never tell you so - have a tough time keeping up with its twists, turns, pitfalls and, to a lesser degree, loopholes. They seem awfully adept at *finding* those, though.

181

Why does your business even need a lawyer?

Consider all of the opportunities your business provides for someone to sue, and you'll begin to get a clear picture. If there seems no need for one, and incorporation and establishment of your business are complete, then perhaps you really don't need one. However, for those of you creating a product, or offering a service that can possibly do bodily harm (even shampoo can burn, in case you've forgotten), then a good attorney should be on retainer – and speed dial.

Are You Willing To Risk It All?

The correct answer, by the way, should be 'no!'

If you answered anything else, then you need a twelve-step gambling program, and a strong cup of coffee.

Being in business, as the previous two sections have mentioned, is risky. There are a lot of unknowns in the world. Some of them come on two legs and are either litigious, or scrupulous to a fault. Either scenario, potentially, spells disaster.

Into this mix, I complete the trifecta of 'professionals you need, who aren't you' with the insurance carrier. Insurance is your way of defending against many unfortunate realities in the cold, cruel world. Theft, acts of nature, accidents, lawsuits, Weird Uncle Pete - all of these are very real, and can affect your business to the point of its ultimate demise.

Why risk all of that?

A good insurance agent should be well established. That's a must, because even though those green ones need business to build their practice, I personally want someone who's been around the block. That's just my personal preference, of course - I don't want to get sued, here.

These agents should also work for a firm, or represent firms, in the case of a brokerage, that meet your specific needs, desires, and policies of social responsibility. I once learned the hard way what a bad insurance agent can do to your pocketbook. And it was expensive in more ways than I care to let on. After that experience, I learned my lesson - sort of. I asked for referrals, and received one from a trusted friend. While his experience with this individual had been 'fine', mine was 'not fine'.

It was at this point, as I was growing older, wiser, and - most importantly - more jaded, that I re-assessed the whole insurance phenomena. I interviewed a few new agents. In the end, I chose the son of a former employer. I chose him not only because I had a good referral, I also chose him because even though he was a Nationally Recognized Top Performer for one of the single largest agencies on the planet, he was also a guy who gave me an hour of his time to answer my questions, and pose his own. This guy was - without a doubt - the guy for me.

To this day, I'm still with this firm, and still in semi-annual contact with my carrier (or more, if need be). The business has since transferred to a new agent, as the old one moved up to VP status in the home office. When this happened, I re-assessed my decision via interview, once more, and felt comfortable with the level of professionalism and clarity that this new agent brought to the table. That happened over a decade ago, and I don't regret a day of it.

Can you say the same?

In the end, insurance needs to be right for you. I actually know that I pay a slightly higher premium than I might with other carriers. I also know, however, that when I am in need of them - 24-7/365.25 - they're there for me.

How?

Because the business I run, coincidentally, has selected the same carrier. And while I've never personally needed them (knocking on major wood, here), the business I work for has.

And you know what?

They were awesome in action. I didn't even need to think. They had professionals for that. In the end, I was covered, safe, and satisfied.

So - for a third and final time - interview, get comfortable, and make sure you choose the carrier who is right for you, with an agent to match. Make sure they understand your needs. Make sure they're privy to your finances, to a degree, so that they may recommend the levels of insurance necessary to keep you out of trouble. A good agent will be able to explain in clear and concise terms *why* you need said insurance in said levels. A great agent will be your partner in business, and call or write now and again to make sure you don't need a checkup. At least, mine does. Does yours?

Computer Health Can Make Or Break Your Business

Would you have random, unprotected sex?

No?

Me either.

So why would you do the same for your computer?

When you run a business, your computer is, oftentimes, at least somewhat involved in the process, if not a component of all of it. So protect it like you would one of your children (okay, to be fair you wouldn't download something to a kid, or put a CD in his/her mouth).

Running a virus scanner and Internet security programs are vital not only to protecting yourself, but protecting those you interact with as well. I remember one instance where a third-party vendor – completely unbeknownst to him – introduced a pair of viruses into a system that I was working on at a former employer. When it was all said and done, the hard drive was toast, and the damage was irrevocable.

Guess whose services we stopped using after that little fiasco?

I personally recommend *Webroot* or *Avast! AVG* is also a decent choice. I've used other major brand names for almost a decade, but now find them too clunky, and prone to flaking out. Also, don't be psyched into buying more than you need.

Want to clean up your computer to get it running like a champ again? *Glary Utilities* can help! It's free, and it's amazing, and you should have it on every PC you own. If you like it, you should also license it.

MalwareBytes is also a must-have piece of the puzzle, as it has a knack for finding things that other software inexplicably miss. Once more, if you like it, you should also license it.

So who am I to tell you these things?

Well, I've been working on PC's for more than 25 years - building them, repairing them, and recovering them. So I've been around the block. But - hey - don't listen to me if you don't want to. Lots of people don't. Talk to your friends. But make sure that they're knowledgeable about the subject. Bad advice can ruin a friendship.

Protect your computer! If you don't, no one else will. And evil-doers world-wide will laugh at you, while pointing and saying nasty things about your Mother. Probably, anyway.

Part 7: The Essential Small Business Bookshelf

Michael Gerber: A Dude You Should Get To Know Better
"The E-Myth Revisited" - Occasionally I will recommend a book to others. I am a voracious reader, and it takes a lot to impress me. This book impressed the hell out of me. It should be read by any and all cottage and small business owners. This is one of those books that - to this day – has proven timeless in its insight and prescience. At its core, it espouses the need for a business to focus on what it does well, and not on random larks that can cause monetary injury or, worse still, a business' demise.

Janet Boydell: A Dude-ette You Need To Learn From
"You're Not The Person I Hired!" - This book is amazing. From the perspective of an employee, from the perspective of a business owner, and from the perspective of a manager: I don't care what the title says, you ALL need to read this book. Twice if need be. Do not hire another single employee until you have done so - it will change the way you think.

Bob Weinstein: Telling It Like It Is
"I Hate My Boss!" - I picked this book up on a lazy afternoon browsing in the local bookstore. Little did I know that so much comprehension of the 'Management' psyche would be laid bare before me. While a great many instances in the book didn't speak to me, I did come to recognize personal shortcomings that I was able to rectify in my own management style and behavior.

Steven R. Covey: A Pioneer In The Now
"The 7 Habits Of Highly Effective People" – I read this book nearly a decade ago. At the time, the manager in me was only beginning to blossom into something recognizable. While I personally found the read a bit dry, and wordy, I nevertheless gleaned some valuable information from it which has stuck with me. I also discovered that many of my personal habits, which I considered overkill to some degree, were, in fact, exactly the right things to be doing. I believe that this book offers something different to all who read it. To all who read it, however, I truly believe there's something powerful in there for you. You need only find it, and then wield it.

Dan Miller: A Resounding Voice In The Business World
"48 Days To The Work You Love" – Loaded with interesting facts, Miller takes us on a journey that begins with quitting your job. While I don't necessarily recommend that for the business owner, what follows will, in fact, make you re-think a great deal (if not all) of what you're doing in life

and – hopefully – allow you to enact meaningful changes that will bring less heartache, headache, and stress, while also bringing more joy and pleasure from your working life.

David Meerman Scott: Someone Who Inpired Me

"The New Rules of Marketing and PR" – When first I began to do research for our future business, I purchased a plethora of works available at the time. Many offered small nuggets of usefulness, but this one brought a little more to the table. This book, among other things, is a great way to understand further how to get more out of social media, and web site, content. While the social media world changes daily, there are still valuable points on offer in this work that, in my opinion, make it a must.

Thomas Stanley: Catharsis In Book Form

"The Millionaire Next Door" – I seldom read books more than once. I have read this one three times, and am about due for a fourth. What Mr. Stanley has done is to outline situational observations about money that are applicable across all walks of life. Within the pages of this work of genius, we discover what wealth really means, who really has it, and how they achieve it. While it may not be useful in your day-to-day operations, its underlying principals are certain to make a lasting – and vibrant – impression upon you, and the life you choose to live.

Ramit Sethi: Simplicity Meets Elegance With A Dash Of Common Sense

"I Will Teach You To Be Rich" – This book brings to bear a great many individual points of light that, when considered as a collective, become a blinding ray of plasma. Throughout its pages, we find that Mr. Sethi challenges us to do the things we know we *should* be doing, but are not. There are excellent sections that outline strategies, wisdom, and everyday tactics that, if nothing else, will make you consider a great many business (and personal) decisions with a lot more care.

Afterword

This book was never meant to be written. I never considered that all of the 'stuff' that I had learned the hard way would be of so much value to so many individuals. What began as a marketing hook for a new business, developed into a series of semi-regular business-related posts on *Facebook* that, inexplicably, developed a cult following.

Over the past three years, since I published this book in its first form, a lot has happened.

First, and foremost, I've become a better writer. I hadn't intended to re-issue this work at all. That was, until I re-opened it (I was looking for a specific passage) and saw what a hot mess it was compared to what sort of product I was putting forth in the here-and-now. Suffice it to say, I felt that I owed it to myself to either discontinue the publication altogether, or to do a full re-write with a new layout. I chose the latter for many reasons. The obvious reason was that writers seem to have an uncanny knack of grossing negative revenue.

The second, and not-so-obvious reason, was that I found myself reminiscing about how much fun I had writing all of those serial 'articles'. As I paged through the work, I was startled to recognize how many of my articles weren't accounted for within it. After dropping them in, I felt like I owed it to myself to give this work a rebirth.

So here we are. I hope you found something in here useful. I hope my mistakes can help prevent you from making the same ones. And most of all, I hope that your business is a success. You've taken a great leap of faith and – success or fail – it's something to be proud of.

Heath D. Alberts
February 10th, 2015

About The Author

Heath D. Alberts is a graduate of Boylan Central Catholic High School, and a college dropout. He has worked in a number of different positions including Insurance Adjudicator & Adjuster, Customer Service, Unix/SS7 mainframe Systems Operator, Web Site Designer, Comic Store Lackey, and Software Support Specialist – to name a few. For the past eighteen years, he has been the Operations Manager of a multi-million dollar area business employing thirty individuals in the highly specialized contract-manufacturing sector.

He is also an experienced house flipper, and the author of numerous other published works and blog series'.

He currently resides in Rockton, Illinois with his amazing wife and business partner, Wanda, and his evil cat who - he's fairly certain - is bent on world domination.

About The Typeface

The majority of the typeface within this book is set in Calibri. It was designed by Lucas De Groot, and released in 2007 to maximize the ClearType rendering technology developed by *Microsoft*. Calibri is defined as a humanist sans-serif typeface beneath the *Microsoft ClearType* Font Collection. It has recently become the de-facto standard for numerous *Microsoft* applications, replacing Times New Roman and Arial. This year, Comic Sans made a valiant coup attempt against Calibri, which resulted in the deaths of several unnamed authors, whose heads imploded at the very sight of the font itself. No one has seen, nor heard from, it since. It is suspected of hiding out in fourth-rate children's books.